THE MARINE
FROM MANDALAY

This is the true story of a Royal Marine wounded by shrapnel in Mandalay who undergoes a long solitary march to flee the Japanese and finds his way back through India to Britain. On his way he has many encounters and adventures and helps British and Indian refugees.

12

THE MARINE
FROM MANDALAY

The Marine From Mandalay

by

James Leasor

Dales Large Print Books
Long Preston, North Yorkshire,
BD23 4ND, England.

British Library Cataloguing in Publication Data.

Leasor, James
    The marine from Mandalay.

    A catalogue record of this book is
    available from the British Library

    ISBN   1-84262-278-1 pbk

Published in Large Print 2003 by arrangement with
House of Stratus

Dales Large Print is an imprint of Library Magna Books Ltd.

Printed and bound in Great Britain by
T.J. (International) Ltd., Cornwall, PL28 8RW

ACKNOWLEDGEMENTS

I would like to acknowledge my debt to the late General Sir Leslie Hollis, KGB, KBE, RM, who first told me the story of William Doyle's experiences in the Second World War. I would also like to thank the following people who helped me in the preparation of this book: Major H B Affleck-Graves, RM, Secretary of the Royal Marine Corps Association; Brigadier Michael Calvert DSO; Mr Alexander J Innes FRCS; Captain A G Newing, RM, Editor, The Globe & Laurel, the Journal of the Royal Marines; and the Archivist and staff of the Royal Marines Museum, Eastney, Hants.

INTRODUCTION

The events with which this story deals happened long ago and far away; in the Second World War, in Burma, but their significance increases with every passing year.

Burma was then a relatively unknown country, and so it still remains. It is one-and-a-quarter times as large as France, three times the size of England, Scotland and Wales put together, but still smaller by several thousand square miles than the state of Texas.

Burma is shaped roughly like a long and narrow hand, fingers pointing south, thumb to the east. The fingers form the delta at the mouth of the Irrawaddy, Burma's greatest river, which rises in the north towards Tibet. The thumb extends more than 300 miles south of Rangoon, the capital, into the Gulf of Martaban, east of the Andaman Islands.

From the southern tip of the country, bordering on Thailand, to its most northerly point in the Kachin Hills, the distance is about 1200 miles, as far as from London to Minsk. At its widest, Burma is 550 miles across. Much of the country is covered by jungle, most of it tropical, with mountain ranges running north to south. The towns are small and widely spaced apart.

Before the Second World War, although a relatively minor country within the British Empire, Burma exported huge amounts of rice every year, was an important producer of high-quality petrol and lubricating oil, and the world's largest source of teak.

In late 1941 it still seemed as though war in Europe and the Middle East would leave all this unchanged. But within months, by the early spring of 1942, the Japanese flag was flying above Singapore, Hong Kong and New Guinea. Malaya had fallen to their forces, Burma was itself all but occupied, and Japanese troops were poised to invade India.

In Europe, meanwhile, the Nazi empire stretched triumphantly from the French Atlantic coast to the Black Sea. From the Mediterranean to the Arctic, Hitler held sway over more than 400 million people. Switzerland was the only remaining European sovereign state between Spain and the Ukraine. In the Middle East the detritus of Allied reverses littered the burning deserts of North Africa.

At this time of disaster and defeat in East and West, with Axis forces seemingly triumphant on every front, General Leslie Hollis, later to be knighted and become Commandant General of the Royal Marines, was Senior Military Assistant Secretary in the Office of the War Cabinet in London. In this capacity, he was in close daily contact with the Prime Minister.

One morning, coming across Mr Churchill in a mood of some depression at this sombre calendar of catastrophe, he attempted to uplift the Premier's spirits by telling him the story of Marine William Doyle in Burma.

Hollis, who had only recently heard it himself from a brother officer in the Royal Marines, felt that it epitomized and encapsulated the virtues of courage, resource and initiative on which the Corps prided itself. When Hollis had finished, Mr Churchill gave his verdict.

'A remarkable tale,' he declared warmly. 'Either the man should have been court-martialled – or he should have received instant promotion and a decoration.'

What had the Marine from Mandalay done that could conceivably deserve either consequence? And what happened to him as a result?

THE MARINE FROM MANDALAY

William Doyle was dreaming. He moved weightlessly, at ease, without care, in that happy half-lit hinterland between sleep and wakefulness. He was in his bed at his parent's home in Mills Street, Middlesbrough, Yorkshire. Through half-closed eyes, he made out the familiar pattern on the wallpaper on the far wall beyond the end of the bed; the photogravure picture above the mantelpiece of a stag standing, antlers raised, on top of a mountain, the equally well-known washstand with china jug and bowl in the corner. Somewhere beyond all these friendly reminders of home, in the world of the fully awake, the factory hooter at Dorman Long, the steel mill at the end of the road, was blaring. The six o'clock shift was about to start; from six o'clock until two in the afternoon and then from two until ten o'clock at night, the two shifts worked six days a week. His father would be there – he was on the early shift – working as a straightener. As the white-hot rolled beams of steel came out of the furnace, he would check them for straightness on a special machine. He had done this as long as

13

William could remember; there was something reassuring in this continuity.

William Doyle could sense rather than feel the nearness of his brother Joseph. Two other brothers, Dennis and John, were sleeping in the room beyond. As the hooter stopped, a clanging of trams began every half-hour, rattling along on their rails, the electrical pick-ups on their roofs sparking against the overhead cables.

Doyle stretched his six-foot-two-inches luxuriously in the warmth, yawned, opened his eyes fully – and was in that instant fully awake.

He was not in his own bed in his familiar room in Middlesbrough, but lying on his back on grass, thick and coarse, of a kind never seen in England. The warmth he felt did not come from the closeness of his brother, but from the sun as it crawled up the burnished sky, pouring heat and a blaze of light through a filter of thick fleshy leaves above his head.

He sat up, shaking his head, wondering whether this was reality or some continuation of his dream. Or could it be what it seemed – a nightmare come to life?

The noises he had mistaken for a factory hooter and a passing tram had no such homely origins. Unseen people were beating a gong, possibly Buddhist monks in a jungle temple. And with this thought came the ultimate realization where he was. The full horror of his predicament hit him like a hammer blow. He was 5000 miles away from home, alone in the centre of the Burmese jungle. The Japanese army was approaching steadily like a creeping tide from south to north. If he did not move, he could be captured, and in that time and place this meant almost certain torture and death.

Doyle stood up, shaking his head to try and rid himself of the panic that erupted in his mind. He was Marine Doyle, No. PLY X100893. Or was he?

Agreed, that was who he had been when he had been part of a proud and highly professional unit, one marine among many, ready to live up to the motto of their Corps, *Per mare, per terram* by sea, by land. Now he was on his own, unarmed, on the run, virtually a refugee. In the middle of the world at war, he was alone, lost, abandoned, betrayed; a man of arms without any weapon – not even a penknife or a sharpened stone; without compass, money, even boots. He was all but naked to a host of advancing enemies.

He was not even wearing uniform. He wore khaki drill shorts, rotting with sweat. His issue khaki shirt had been torn to shreds by thorns in the jungle, and had swiftly deteriorated to a mass of ragged shreds of cloth. He had found an empty sugar bag in a looted warehouse and cut holes in this for his head and his arms. He did not have a hat of any kind to protect his head against the ferocious heat of a perpendicular noonday sun. His feet and ankles had been badly cut by shrapnel in the last action in which he had been involved. The wounds had turned septic, and had been bound with bandages, now filthy and soaked with pus. It was impossible to squeeze any boots over these sodden bandages. So Doyle stood barefoot in the jungle.

How had he ever got into this extraordinary and bizarre situation?

Certainly little in his childhood had any bearing on his present situation or relevance to it. He left St Patrick's School in Middlesbrough when he was 14, then served for a time as a butcher's boy working for the Middlesbrough Co-operative Society. In this capacity, he had ridden a bicycle with a big wheel at the back, a small one in front and above this a metal tray where the packets of meat he had to deliver were wrapped up with a tiny skewer through each one, with a tag giving the name and address of the person to whom he had to deliver it.

He worked there for two years, but when the master butcher wanted him to go to night school several evenings a week to learn how to cut the various joints, how to make beef olives, how to mark out a sirloin, Doyle had told him he wasn't interested.

16

'I was daft as a brush,' Doyle would admit later. 'I should have learned while I had the chance.' As he was discovering now, chances often come unannounced and can pass unrecognized. It struck him that his life so far was rather like this trek through the jungle, set on a one-way course. He could stop or he could go on; he could never go back.

After refusing to attend night school, Doyle had to resign. He was out of work for a fortnight and then someone in the Co-op asked whether he would care to go 'on the milk'. This meant delivering milk every morning to upwards of a hundred homes. For the first few weeks he pushed a barrow packed with milk bottles in wire cages, one cage stacked on another. Then he progressed to a horse and cart. This was a little more exciting and a lot less effort. Sometimes the horse was frisky; if they passed a steamroller in the road or a very noisy motorcycle, it would rear up and bolt and drag the cart all the way to Stewart's Park, past the dairy, right up to the site of Captain Cook's Museum.

Occasionally the horse took the bit between its teeth and careered along at such a rate that the cart turned over and all the bottles would be smashed. On other mornings the horse would be quite docile; it knew the daily routine better than Doyle; after all, it had been doing it longer. Stop at

17

one house, pass three, stop at the fourth, go on to the seventh, and so on. Once, in a cul-de-sac, he had to turn the cart around, and the horse suddenly took fright at something, a bird or a car backfiring, and backed the cart into a house window.

At the time it seemed that the months spent walking milk rounds, up and down long streets, in and out of front gardens, were of no value beyond providing him with a wage. In fact, these miles of walking in all weathers, hot, cold and wet, provided a discipline that later he would remember with gratitude.

Life was casual then, thought Doyle now as he began to walk through the jungle, head down, each step an agony. Events tended to go at the pace of the horse, whereas for weeks now there was urgency behind him, the pressure of pursuit, where capture meant the unthinkable, an abandonment not only of liberty, but of hope.

On the morning of 3 September, a Sunday, William Doyle was delivering the milk to one house just after 11 o'clock when the housewife came out and said, without any greeting, 'War's broken out'. This was not unexpected, but the moment of its arrival, with the almost immediate wail of an air-raid siren, had the quality of finality. Doyle instinctively knew that from that moment on nothing would ever be quite the same again.

Next morning, when he was going home from work to have his midday meal, he decided to join up. He passed a recruiting office in the Wesley Hall in Linthorpe Road, looked at the photographs in the window of tanks and planes and ships, and decided he would volunteer for the Navy.

It seemed better to volunteer than wait to be called up. If he waited, he might not have the chance to join the service he wanted, but would be drafted wherever the need for recruits was greatest. Inside the hall were four desks with a pile of forms on each, extolling the attractions of the Royal Marines, the Royal Navy, the Army, the Royal Air Force. A Marines sergeant was standing at the door.

'What can we do for you, son?' he asked him cheerfully.

When Doyle told him he was planning to join the Navy, the sergeant shook his head.

'A big smart fellow like you shouldn't be joining the Navy,' he told him. 'You should be joining the Marines.'

Until then, Doyle had no idea what a marine was; he had never seen one in Middlesbrough. The sergeant, however, was wearing a smart blue uniform with red stripes down the seams of the trousers. This outfit certainly looked more attractive than the bell-bottoms of a matelot, with a flap that opened instead of fly-buttons, so Doyle asked him: 'If I join the Marines, do I get a uniform like yours?'

'Yes, of course,' replied the sergeant enthusiastically. 'Bags of action, bags of good grub, girls everywhere. And more, much more!'

Just how much more, at least in the way of experience, Doyle later discovered.

This sounded such an agreeable prospect to Doyle that he made up his mind at once.

'I'll join the Marines then,' he said, and signed the form.

Two friends, Ted Porter and Joe Duggan, were milkmen with him, and they called into the Wesley Hall later that day and also joined the Marines. Within a week Doyle received his travel warrant and papers to report to the Marines' headquarters in Plymouth. At Plymouth station a sergeant mustered a number of young men in civilian suits, sports jackets and flannels, porkpie hats, flat caps, or no hats at all, who came off the train. They were bundled into trucks and driven to Stonehouse Barracks, just off Union Street.

The centre of Plymouth did not impress Doyle. Coming from the industrial bustle of Middlesbrough, his first impression was that it was old-fashioned and small. The barracks were large, however, and entered through a high stone archway. Here Doyle was given his number – X100893 – with the prefix PLY for Plymouth. Marines joining up at Deal had the prefix DEA. Portsmouth Marines came off worst: their code prefix was simply POX.

Doyle was there for six months, then at Fort Cumberland, where he became a member of the Mobile Naval Base Defence Organization. This involved being taught how to rig a huge tripod with a rope and pulleys so that two or three men could pick up and move a six-inch gun barrel and swing it around easily. The idea was that if they were posted abroad to a naval base and ships came in with guns shattered after a battle at sea, the Marines detachment would be able to winch the damaged barrels ashore and replace them.

Doyle could never imagine in what strange and unexpected circumstances this training would prove the means, not of taking lives, but of saving many – including his own – or when and how he would next march beneath the arch outside the barracks.

After a week's embarkation leave, he sailed in a convoy from Greenock, taking both Arctic and tropical kit – either in an attempt to deceive any enemy agents, or because there was genuine doubt about their destination. When the ships reached Freetown in West Africa and lay offshore, the Arctic gear was stored in the hold. They sailed on to Durban, then up the east coast of Africa. The troopship was an adapted Norwegian liner, with a crew of Norwegians and Canadians. One morning a message on the tannoy asked for volunteers to help the cooks in the galley. This seemed to Doyle and several others more agreeable than being up on deck doing repeated lifeboat drill, falling in, falling out, manning guns, aiming but not firing at imaginary targets, or squatting on the after deck out of the wind and the smoke from the funnels for a quick cigarette and a game of cards. In the galley there could be the chance of some extra food to supplement the dreary meals of corned-beef mash and mugs of tea, for which they queued with mess tins, to be eaten on mess decks crammed with men.

At night the floor of each mess deck was spread with blankets and, above the blankets, rows of hammocks were slung. If someone in a high hammock had drunk too much in the wet canteen, he might vomit on the man who lay beneath him, or if his bladder was weak and he was unable to reach the heads, he would urinate like an aerial fountain. Because every porthole was screwed shut with a steel cover over it throughout the hours of darkness, and every door had blackout curtains, the smell of sweat and food and urine did not add to appetite.

In the galley at least the lights were bright, there was always plenty of sweet, hot tea and maybe a couple of fried eggs on the side.

Most of the work was classed as spud-bashing; each volunteer squatted on an unturned bucket and with a sharp knife peeled potatoes from one pile and then threw them on another.

The head chef was Norwegian, and at the end of each shift he would show his thanks by giving his helpers half a chicken out of one of the ship's giant refrigerators, or a pound of butter, or maybe a loaf of bread. Then they would go to the wet canteen, pool their pay, buy a bottle of gin and sleep off their meal in the spud locker. This wasn't exactly the life that the recruiting sergeant in the smart blue uniform had promised, but at least it was survival, and more pleasant than life on a stinking mess deck.

One day a Canadian sailor drank too much red biddy, a rough raw concoction of methylated spirits, gin, whisky and rum, and died. It was announced on the tannoy he would be buried at sea. On the night before this committal, after hours peeling potatoes, Doyle asked the Norwegian cook what they could have to eat.

The cook replied: 'Go down to the main fridge and get yourself a chicken – there's a mass in there. One'll never be missed.'

So Doyle and a messmate went down into the deep recesses of the vessel, until they were in a hold where the grey walls glistened perpetually with condensation, like sweat, and the thunder of the propeller blades beat like drums in their ears. As landsmen, they were uneasily aware that they were now thirty, forty, maybe fifty feet beneath the surface of the sea. If the ship was torpedoed, they were dead men. The weather was rough and the ship literally curved under the immense pressure of the waves. Looking along the corridor, they could see it flex from one end to the other as the ship rose and fell and rolled from side to side, as though weary of the waves but quite unable to escape them.

They came to the main refrigerator, big as a room, and opened the double doors. A cold puff of frozen fog blew out in their faces. Under a blaze of shielded lights, they could see racks of food, all covered by white sheets. They peered in and lifted away the nearest sheet to reach a chicken. Instead, inches from their eyes were two bare feet, blue and cold with death. The corpse of the dead sailor was being kept in the fridge because of the heat outside.

'Somehow, after that, we didn't feel like chicken,' said Doyle later. We didn't feel like anything except to get the hell out.'

The ship reached Port Suez, south of the Suez Canal, and the marines went to a transit camp for two weeks to become acclimatised. From the train taking them from the docks to this camp, they saw lines of Egyptians squatting, defecating in the sand by the side of the railway. Others were standing up to urinate, and when they saw the pale faces peering out of the train windows, they directed their flow at them as a mark of their hatred for the effendi.

'And these are the blokes we're supposed to be ready to die for,' said one of Doyle's colleagues in disgust.

'Speak for yourself,' replied Doyle dourly.

One of their duties in camp was to man the telephone exchange, with duty watches every two hours, day and night. The exchange had a complex switchboard, with plugs that needed to be slotted into sockets when tiny lids dropped over the numbers being dialled.

One of the marines in the draft came from Ashby de la Zouch in Leicestershire. He had the nickname Ash, partly because not everyone had heard of Ashby de la Zouch. (This was before the song made it famous.) Then they called him Crash Ash because he seemed to have difficulty in keeping his balance, and appeared unco-ordinated. He would fall over, trip up, and sometimes did not seem to understand a simple order. If it could be got wrong, Crash Ash would get it wrong. One night everything went wrong.

Doyle had come off the early morning watch, six o'clock to eight, and was just getting his head down when he heard a loud report, like an explosion, from the direction of the telephone exchange. Crash Ash was rolling about on the floor, holding his hands to his face, screaming, thrashing his legs in agony. Blood was trickling through his fingers.

Later Doyle heard what had happened. With no calls to place, and time on his hands, Ash had opened the drawer of a desk in this office and found a curious white object like a pigeon's egg with two wires protruding from it. With nothing better to do, he idly stuck these two wires like prongs into the telephone sockets. He could hardly have found anything worse to do, for the current charged through the sockets and exploded the egg which blew both eyes out of his head. The 'egg' was a detonator, waiting for an explosion.

Some days later, forty Royal Marines were taken down to Port Suez and loaded aboard a ship, the *City of Canterbury*. At the top of the gangway stood an orderly, handing out wills to each man as he went aboard. In the back of every service paybook, the AB64 in the Army, a will is already printed, and any requests can be filled in with the soldier's signature, but here all paybooks had been left behind because they were going into action. But where, or what? No one seemed to know. At least, no one told them.

The crew were Lascars and the ship was

old and showed her age as she lumbered north into the Mediterranean. Three times they came under air attack. They had Bren guns and rifles to fire at the aircraft, but soon discovered the value of shooting .303 bullets against dive-bombers travelling at nearly 300 miles an hour.

In the middle of the third attack, the ship's engine stopped. The *City of Canterbury* wallowed uselessly, a metal hulk in the shining sea. The marines were not particularly concerned about what they were expected to do now because it was clear they could do nothing but endure their predicament. They managed to find some beer in the canteen, but this was in a keg and had to be poured into a bucket into which they dipped mugs. The beer, after all this, turned out to be flat, but it was better than the brackish drinking water. After a day and a half the engine was restarted, but they were too late for whatever action had been planned, so now they put about and sailed south at half-speed.

They next went to Ismailia on the Sinai side of the Canal to join a group of Australian soldiers guarding an airfield. They were told that, since Crete had fallen, the Germans might drop parachutists in an attempt to seize the airfield and then the Canal. The marines dug slit trenches at each end of the runway and, since it was accepted that if parachutists landed in the dark no one would know friend from foe, the marines had to wear armbands on their right arms to differentiate them from any invaders.

Every evening, tommy-guns in their hands, they would climb into these slit trenches and wait. There were no sirens to give the alarm, but two searchlights at the end of the Canal were used to give a silent warning of the approach of any enemy aircraft. When the beams of these lights would cross in the night sky, the marines knew a raid was on the way.

But although there were many such air-raid alarms, there were no air raids. Night after night the marines and Australians climbed into their trenches; morning after morning they climbed out again. They slept in tents during the daylight hours, on strips of wood from packing cases. This was marginally more comfortable than simply lying on the sand, which would work its way into their boots, trousers, sleeves and underpants, giving the feeling, when the wind blew, of having their entire flesh sandpapered.

One evening they climbed into the trenches as usual and waited for several hours. The searchlights stayed dark. At midnight an officer blew his whistle.

'Get back to bed,' he told them. 'Nothing's going to happen tonight.'

Thankfully they climbed out of the gritty trenches and went back to their packing-case beds. As Doyle lay under the thin canvas of his tent, he heard the drone of approaching aircraft.

'I wonder where they are?' someone asked drowsily in the hot darkness.

They must be our lot,' someone else replied. They're coming in from two directions.'

Doyle thought this unusual, because there were no planes on the airfield and none were expected. The airfield was empty of all Allied aircraft; it was simply a landing place, ringed by hangars packed with stores.

The next thing he remembered was waking up and staring at stars that stared back unwinkingly at him. His tent had disappeared and the ground was shaking with the tremor of massive explosions. Flames leapt with long yellow tongues all around the airfield.

The planes they had heard were now coming in so low they could see the swastika markings on their fuselages by the light of the fires. Cannon shells poured into all the perimeter buildings. Every fifth shell was a tracer, like a red shooting star, to mark the target.

The marines raced out, some naked and barefoot, others wearing underpants or swimming trunks or PT shorts, with boots unlaced. They leapt into their slit trenches and sprayed the sky with tommy-gun

29

bullets. This was quite useless, purely a token reaction. The aircraft disappeared over the horizon and left them to a scene of chaos. Crates of spares had been machine-gunned and their contents ruined. Next morning the airfield was littered with bodies of RAF ground crew. Some had feverishly attempted to dig shallow holes in the ground and, when bombs dropped close by, they had been buried alive. They had literally dug their own graves.

From then on, night after night, just as the sky was growing dark, the searchlights would cross in their warning X, and more German bombers appeared. A surprising number of the bombs they dropped did not explode. The airstrips were soon marked with their metal fins sticking up from the sand.

These regular raids continued for three weeks and then the RAF air crews, who had no planes to fly and whose continued presence there was therefore unnecessary, were marched out through the perimeter wire to bivouac several miles away in the desert.

The marines stayed in their trenches. Several were wounded, some seriously, and when one marine was killed by a lump of falling shrapnel, the sergeant formed them up to march to safer positions away from the target. At that moment the evening raid, the heaviest so far, began. Fires began to blaze all around the airfield. Under the full

Egyptian moon Doyle could see the planes in silhouette. The roar and rush of slipstream blew their hats from their heads.

While this was going on, the sergeant started to march them off, shouting, 'Left! Left! Left, right, left! Keep up in the back there', as though they were back on the drill square in Plymouth. Those in the back took his advice too literally. They started to run, pushing into those in front of them. Within seconds the platoons were in shambles, the sergeant calling out, 'Come back! Come back, there!' No one obeyed but everyone found shelter of some sort. Doyle curled himself around a date tree. Others dug themselves shallow pits in the sand and waited for morning. Then the sergeant walked up and down the nearest road, blowing his whistle. Out of the sand, like creatures rising from some phantasmagorical dream, the marines sheepishly came back on parade.

Orders now arrived to construct a dummy airfield some miles away, with huts and dumps of petrol cans that would hopefully draw the pilots off the real target. The marines cut barrage balloons in half and fitted them up across strips of cane so that from the air they would resemble makeshift hangars. Empty petrol cans were piled up with any other junk that could be found, and a few old tents erected on the perimeter to make it look as much like an airfield as possible. When it was complete they left to spend the night in the desert nearby. Some stayed behind to start small fires when the bombers appeared, to draw them towards the false target.

The Luftwaffe ignored this subterfuge and continued to direct their attentions to the main airfield. When the marines went out the following morning the dummy airfield had vanished: local Arabs had come in the night and removed everything.

On the wider scene of war, the Japanese attacked Pearl Harbor and Singapore in December, 1941. The marines, a draft now of more than 400, sailed off in an armed merchant cruiser, but again had no idea of their destination or what their duties would be. The ship's deck was packed with invasion barges, so it seemed reasonable to assume they were going to invade, but where or what or when?

One morning they awoke to a silent stationary ship. The engines had stopped. The thumping of the propeller and the rumble of the long propeller shaft had ceased. They went up on deck and saw, only a few hundred yards away, a tropical island, with palm trees and surf breaking on a bone-white beach. This instantly brought back memories of films starring Dorothy Lamour and Betty Grable. Their escort vessels included *Ark Royal* and the two cruisers

Dorsetshire and *Cornwall.* Other ships on the convoy were carrying scaffolding and trucks and earth movers and mechanical diggers. All had stopped with them. Was this their destination? No one even knew what it was, or where it was, and there appeared no sign of life or habitation. They waited for two days while parties went ashore to check whether the Japanese were already in occupation. They weren't, so the invasion barges were lowered and engines started. The marines climbed down rope ladders and scrambling nets into them. The barges made short obligatory circuits of the ship to warm up their engines and headed for the island.

A coral reef a hundred yards out from the shore prevented them running up the beach. The water was too shallow to take the draught of the barges, so everyone had to jump out and wade ashore. When they came to unload trucks and other vehicles, they roped them with pulleys to palm trees and hoisted them in. Now Doyle realized the value of the exercise of the tripod and old gun barrels at Fort Cumberland.

Up from the beach, between the shore and the line of trees and jungle, stood a stockade of pointed stakes. Over these stakes, rows of dark faces watched the new arrivals. From the sea it appeared as though these heads were actually impaled on the stakes, in the way that heads of felons executed at Tyburn

33

long ago used to be put on public view as a warning to any others inclined to break the law. But they were only the heads of inquisitive islanders, who lived in huts behind the stakes. They had no idea who the marines were: it seemed doubtful to Doyle whether they even realized the world was at war. It was only then that the marines were told they had landed in the Maldive Islands. Until then they had never heard of this rash of small islands or atolls, tossed like a necklace into the middle of the Indian Ocean.

They moved among the villagers, attempting to introduce themselves – and moved back very smartly. Everyone appeared to be suffering from elephantiasis. Their legs were swollen to the thickness of a healthy man's body; thighs rubbed together as they walked. There was something horrible about the sight; Doyle felt he had arrived on an island inhabited by bizarre misshapen freaks. Neither he, nor any of the draft, had ever seen so many people so horribly deformed.

'I didn't fancy walking down Linthorpe Road with legs like that,' said Doyle dryly.

Was the disease infectious? How did one catch it? Through drinking water? Eating unwashed fruit? The marines were all for climbing back aboard, but this was impossible. In an effort to reassure them, the captain of *Cornwall* now came ashore. He called everyone together on the beach, stood on a packing case, and addressed them all.

'I want to tell you men that this is a disease that only affects the locals,' he declared, without totally convincing his audience. There's no evidence – that I know of, at least – that any *white* man has ever caught elephantiasis.'

There was a pause. The marines mumbled among themselves. What basis had the captain for this statement? Had he any basis at all? But they did not raise these questions, because between the rank of marine and naval captain in the year 1942 there was a great gulf fixed, not notably less than that between Lazarus and Dives in the Bible story.

'On the other hand,' the captain went on, 'I would like to give you this advice. Don't walk about barefoot. Keep your boots on. Just in case.'

When they bathed in the sea, the more cautious marines wore canvas gym shoes in case the sharp coral cut their feet and their legs swelled to these appalling proportions.

They were ordered to cut roads through the jungle, but in making them they discovered that the earth was little more than two feet thick. A few inches beneath the surface it degenerated into thick damp mud, and beneath this lay hard coral.

They also discovered that others had been there before them, and indeed were still there. The Maldive Islanders apparently had the custom of hollowing out tree trunks and into these they laid the bodies of their dead. They could only use these shallow graves because the coral was so hard it resisted all their efforts to dig into it. So when the heavy trucks and bulldozers moved in, they were soon churning up bones and skulls.

The headman – what rank he held, the marines did not know, but they nicknamed him the Prime Minister – was rowed about in a canoe from atoll to atoll. He sat in the stern, a sombre impassive figure, his face shaded from the sun by a large yellow umbrella. There was considerable argument about what had happened with the trucks. As Doyle put it: 'I don't think he went a bundle on us messing up his cemetery.' But unfortunately, what was done could not be undone.

The feelings of the islanders were made very plain and Doyle realized the folly of antagonizing people whose friendship and loyalty could be of paramount importance – an avoidable situation which in the months ahead he was going to encounter again, and even more sharply. The marines did their best to be friendly, but they had nothing to offer the islanders; no sweets, few cigarettes, not even a common language. Eventually they finished the camp and set up two four-inch guns at each end of the atoll and a six-inch gun in the middle.

They used the scaffold poles carried on another ship to construct a 90-foot tower, on top of which the islanders built a hut of bamboos. In this hut marines kept watch day and night with a rangefinder. One morning Doyle was on duty in his lookout post and far on the horizon, possibly 20 miles away, he could see smudges of smoke. Ships were approaching – but whose, friends' or foes'?

He had been given a handbell to ring as warning if he sighted any vessels, and he rang this furiously.

The gun crews stood by, piles of shells near their guns, as gradually the smoke resolved into the outline of a vast ship, and *Prince of Wales,* one of the largest warships in the Navy, sailed towards them. The marines were thankful this was not a Japanese vessel of similar size. The six-inch gun on the island, with its range of perhaps five miles, would have been useless against the guns of a capital ship that could search them out at five times this range.

The *Prince of Wales* dropped anchor and Admiral Tom Phillips, commanding the fleet, which also included *Repulse,* on their way to Singapore, came ashore. The crew brought supplies of bread and flour for the garrison, who were very short of such items. Their only source of safe drinking water was a converter on the beach. Sea water was pumped into this and passed through chemicals, and then fresh water, or at least unsalted water, trickled from a pipe on the other side of the machine. This allowed the men half a pint each a day for washing and drinking.

The island was riddled with mosquitoes, and Doyle, with others, went down with malaria. An area had been cleared for a hospital built from flattened bamboo poles. The treatment for malaria was limited to massive doses of quinine. Since the men's rations were hard biscuits, this brought on immediate vomiting. Sleeping in cots made of bamboo and coconut fibre, the malaria victims, delirious with high temperatures, thrashed about so violently they had to be bound to their beds to restrain them.

Scrub typhus broke out, and skin complaints, thought to be from poisoned coral, became almost universal. Small cuts and grazes became septic and wept matter and other liquid. Finally so many men were totally incapacitated that a hospital ship came out from Ceylon and took the worst cases back to Colombo for treatment. While there, news came that *Prince of Wales* and *Repulse* had both been sunk off the Malayan coast. Some survivors from *Prince of Wales* arrived in Ceylon and were billeted with convalescing marines in a camp in the hills above Colombo. This camp was technically known as a rest camp and had little discipline. Many of the sailors and marines had not been paid for weeks, some not for months. As a result, it was decided that such men could receive as much pay as was due, from entries in their paybooks, in lump sums. This money was largely spent on drink. The result was unfortunate.

'There was a fight one night,' says Doyle. 'The navy fought the marines. The marines fought the army. The locals fought them all. Next morning, in general assembly, a master-at-arms addressed us.

'"I've seen all you tough guys fighting, showing how tough you are," he said. "Let's see how you face some *proper* fighting. I want a hundred volunteers for a special task – helping the navy."'

Within minutes he had two hundred volunteers and slimmed these down to one hundred. No one knew what they were supposed to do; again, no one told them anything except that they were now a unit with the name Force Viper.

They were issued with new rifles, taken down in trucks to Colombo and marched aboard the cruiser *Enterprise*.

Everyone had to take their share of duties with the crew. Ten sailors were normally in the magazine, and now they received as many marines to work with them. Doyle calculated from the positions of the stars that they were steaming in a north-easterly direction. The men on his mess deck were listening to the ship's radio, tuned into a BBC news bulletin. This contained news that Rangoon had just fallen to the Japanese.

They sat staring at each other in disbelief. Hong Kong, Singapore, *Prince of Wales, Repulse,* and now Rangoon. Was there no way to stop the Japanese advance? Ten minutes later, as they discussed the matter, a sergeant came into the mess deck.

'Attention, everyone. Marines detachment, Force Viper,' he said, 'Prepare to land in Rangoon in the morning.'

'But it has just fallen.' Doyle told him. 'It was on the news.'

'I don't care about that news. This is *my* news – and these are your orders.'

The marines were astonished at this reply. What was the point of landing if the city had already fallen? It seemed that they would be going into certain and instant captivity. Not even Doyle's experiences in futility, of turning back from an unknown target in the Mediterranean, defending an indefensible airfield, or contracting malaria in the Maldives, had prepared him for the task ahead. Or, in a sense, perhaps they had. Perhaps, like odd and isolated pieces of a jigsaw, they combined to form a mosaic of war.

No one could amplify the order and no one would countermand it. At dawn the marines lashed Bren guns and tommy-guns to the handrails of the ship as they steamed up the river towards Rangoon. At first the banks were low on either side and dotted with villages. In the distance gleamed the gold cone shape of the Shwe Dagon pagoda. The banks now were lined with warehouses, godowns and office buildings.

Above them Japanese Zero fighters dived and swooped. The anti-aircraft guns of the *Enterprise,* with her Oerlikon and Bofors guns, chattered away, spraying out hot shell-cases across the deck, but the aircraft soared away undamaged.

The order was explicit: field service marching order was to be worn and detachment to land in Rangoon immediately. On the mess deck the marines picked up their packs and water bottles, webbing pouches for extra Bren gun magazines and tin helmets. These were of quaint design with metal visors which folded down to protect their eyes from blast and the glare of the sun. They were based on a design first described by Marco Polo in the 14th century and had small slits through which the wearer could see. The thinking behind this headgear was that the visor would protect the face to some extent and also minimize the effect of direct sunlight, which could dazzle and even blind. A quarter-master sergeant issued them with K-ration tins stamped with the contents: soya links, dehydrated potatoes, biscuits, a tube of sweetened condensed milk, a bar of chocolate in a heatproof wrapping. He also issued each man with a large knife.

'What's this for, to open tins?' asked Doyle.

'Funny, eh?' retorted the sergeant. 'It's to cut the head off a bloody snake if it bites you.'

'What happens if it bites before I can cut its head off?'

'Then you got to get down and suck the poison out of the wound.'

'What if it's a place we can't reach, Sarge?'

'Get your best mucker to do it for you. Ask a bloody silly question, you get a bloody silly answer.'

The hundred volunteers, under Major Duncan Johnston, with Captain Herbert Alexander, Lieutenant Douglas Fayle, Lieutenant Peter Cave, Lieutenant Alexander Innes, the Medical Officer, and Sergeant Scott stood ready to leave the ship.

With Japanese aircraft controlling the skies, and according to the radio news, Japanese troops already commanding the city, their task was presumably to be one of sabotage. Perhaps they were to blow up the huge oil storage tanks at Syriam nearby, where tens of millions of gallons of aviation spirit and vehicle petrol were stored, or maybe destroy telephone exchanges, bring back secret papers, bullion from a bank? The assignment must surely be one that could be described as an in/out affair. Rumours abounded, but nobody seemed to know.

Scrambling nets, carried rolled up on the sides of the ship, were now cut loose. The marines climbed down them into small boats which had been lowered against the reassuring cliff-like side of *Enterprise*. These boats bobbed and ducked like coracles, toy paddle boats in a seaside pleasure lake.

'Better you than me, mate!'... 'Keep your heads down and knees together,' shouted sailors watching them climb into the boats. The marines shouted back their answers, but ribaldry could not mask the doubts they felt.

They consoled themselves with the thought that their task would be swift; then it would be back aboard again.

They crouched down in the boats. Engines fired. No circling of the ship this time, just straight into the shore. A hundred yards off the docks, Doyle turned round.

'Look at that!' he cried.

Everyone in his boat turned and looked in the direction of his pointing finger. To their total astonishment, almost disbelief, *Enterprise* had turned in the river, and was sailing full steam south.

'She's left us! What the bloody hell's going on?'

'Eyes front,' said the sergeant. 'Stand by to disembark.'

'But how are we going to get away when we've done our job? And what is our job?'

No one answered. There was no answer. A hundred and five Royal Marines, officers and men, were about to land from three motor boats on the docks of an Empire capital apparently already in enemy hands. Behind this city lay a country already all but conquered, and to the south Malaya, Singapore, Hong Kong were totally occupied. What could Force Viper possibly achieve? What was the aim, the intention? Unease gripped their stomachs like fists.

The boats ran alongside a concrete quay. Marines made them fast against hanging motor tyres and rope buffers. Even in this situation, their training, to avoid damaging the paintwork of any craft, was followed. The men scrambled out, stretching their legs on land, looking about them.

Major Johnston addressed them.

'Our job here is to help the Burma navy,' he said.

We didn't even know they got a navy, sir,' said Doyle.

'Possibly said the Major, 'but they have. They've got these three launches here for a start.'

He indicated three long vessels in smart white paint, with their names, *Rita*, *Stella*,

44

and *Doris* in gold on their bows. Each launch had a Vickers machine-gun mounted up forward. These guns sat on a tripod and had a tank of water to cool the barrel on one side. They required two men to use. One had the task of feeding in a belt of cartridges, while his colleague aimed and fired the gun. This was of a design already old in the First World War and not calculated to induce confidence in its users more than a quarter of a century later.

'What are we to do in these launches, sir?' asked Doyle.

'Seek out the enemy.'

That shouldn't be hard,' said someone dryly.

The marines looked about them; an eerie silence hung over the docks like an evil miasma. They could not see anyone within the complex, service or civilian, friend or foe. Cranes stood curved like the great beaks of huge, listening, wary birds. Water lapped against vertical moss-covered stakes on the edge of the quay. The sheds seemed empty. Several cars were parked in a haphazard way. Some even had doors and luggage boot lids open, as though drivers had left in such a hurry, or in such danger, they had neither time nor inclination to close them.

The atmosphere reminded Doyle of the steelworks in Middlesbrough on a Bank Holiday. Nothing was working, no one was

45

on duty. The marines moved carefully from one godown to another. All were deserted, but crammed with stores. On the docks stood piles of crates marked *Ammunition, Supplies, This Way Up, Handle With Care*. But no one was there to read these instructions, to unpack the guns, spares and ammunition they contained. The docks were dead and deserted, and so, for the moment, was the city.

On Christmas Day a hundred Japanese bombers and fighters had raided Rangoon, which did not possess an early warning system. The only warning of this mass air attack was given by men posted up in trees around the perimeter holding wooden rattles in their hands, of the sort used by partisan supporters at football matches. As soon as they saw the aircraft approaching, they swung these rattles around their heads and gave the alarm. But by then the planes were already over Rangoon, their task accomplished and on the way back to base.

They left 1250 dead; at least that was the number of bodies police counted in the streets and in ruined buildings. The true total was undoubtedly higher. Six hundred more people died from their injuries in the crowded hospitals. The Burmese did not relish the idea of going down into primitive underground shelters without lights or ventilation; this seemed to them unpleasantly like entering a mass grave before death.

The British in Burma, as elsewhere, had been conditioned to believe that the Japanese were good copiers of other countries' ideas, but not to be taken too seriously as adversaries. They were said to have poor eyesight. They all wore thick-lensed spectacles, didn't they? So how could the Japanese possibly make good fighter and bomber pilots? This complacency cost many their lives, and more all their belongings and their livelihoods. Most had read about the German blitz in Britain; they did not believe such a situation could ever obtain in Burma.

This first air raid shattered such comfortable and comforting beliefs. Everyone who could leave Rangoon left, including many who should have stayed. They went in cars, laden down on the springs with suitcases, with trunks, kitchen tables and extra cans of petrol lashed to the roof. They left on motorcycles, by cycles, by bullock carts, on horseback; on foot, pushing their belongings in barrows, handcarts, children's prams. There was no plan in their leaving, only the basic human urge to survive somewhere, anywhere. They wanted to escape before Japanese bombers came over for a second time.

There was only one way to go – north – up the main road, towards the aerodrome at Mingaladon, 12 miles out of the city.

Farther north lay the assumed safety of other more distant towns: Pegu, Prome, Mandalay. Surely the Japs could not pursue them such distances?

Because Rangoon was by then almost empty, casualties in the next air raid were relatively small: 60 civilians killed, 40 wounded. This raid cut the arteries and nerves of the city. Trains stood derelict on their rails, abandoned by drivers and conductors. Postmen did not deliver letters. In any case, the people to whom they were addressed were no longer at their addresses. Telephone exchanges stopped work. The sewage system broke down. Hotels, offices, houses, blocks of flats were without water or electricity. A strong stench of sewage poisoned the air.

Indian shopkeepers put up their shutters. Looters smashed them down again and raided the shops of all they could carry away. People hammered on the doors of banks, desperate to withdraw money, perhaps all their savings, to use on the journey north. Others crowding around bank doors pathetically and paradoxically believed that the banks still offered a place of safety to deposit what items they could salvage. But many local bank employees had fled. Some European managers locked the vaults and followed them.

In the large hotels, such as the Silver Grill,

the Savoy and the Strand, cooks stayed on duty with managers and other clerical staff for as long as they had food to serve. Waiters had gone. Guests queued up in the kitchen for meals. The washing-up hands had disappeared, and bedrooms, kitchens, dining-rooms were littered with piles of dirty plates, cups, saucers, glasses.

Men of the Gloucestershire Regiment worked as butchers, drivers and labourers, helping to unload ships, or repair bomb damage to the airfields. Locally enlisted troops were very ill-equipped for war. Officers, mostly pre-war company executives, were without ammunition for their revolvers. A tommy-gun was allotted to each infantry section, but without ammunition. They had no compasses, tin hats or medical supplies, not even, in many cases, first field dressings, simply basic wads of gauze and bandage which fitted into a special pocket of uniform trousers. These troops looked the part of soldiers but, through lack of ammunition, they were more like actors in a make-believe defence force.

The marines went into the nearest building on the docks, which was packed to the roof with wooden crates. Some had been prised open with crowbars to see what they contained and, when the looters found they contained machinery, they had abandoned them in search of more marketable items.

In another building they found a dozen Burmese civilians sitting around a table with glasses and mugs in front of them. They were drinking rum, whisky, gin, and looked up at the new arrivals without surprise. A liquor store had been broached and these bottles extracted. They invited the marines to join them, but the offer was easy to decline. There was something macabre about the scene: they were like mourners at the funeral of a nation – and the approach of the Japanese army could mean their own demise.

These men told the marines stories of lack of equipment and, more important, lack of resolve. Some were apparently in the Burma navy, but none wore uniform. A few wore white duck trousers and short-sleeved shirts, but more had gone back to the safe *longyi*, the native Burmese dress for men, a long skirt-like garment wound around their waist. In these they would not stand out as men who had associated with Europeans. However, they were perfectly friendly and willing to help the marines if they could do so.

'What we need,' the Major explained, 'are sheets of metal plate to weld round the rails of these launches, otherwise anyone on deck is a sitting target. Have you got any sheet metal here?'

'Of course,' said someone. He gave an order to some other men, who left the table and returned dragging long rusty metal plates along the ground; they were too heavy and unwieldy to lift. Someone else brought an oxygen cylinder, a welding torch, goggles and gloves.

They came out on to the docks and began to weld this armour in place around the decks of the three launches. The marines were able to manhandle drums of diesel to fill up the tanks; others brewed up tea. A store was opened to provide sugar, tea, tins of milk.

No one seemed to have any definite news, but the air was thick with rumour. The broadcast announcement that Rangoon had fallen was only partly true. The suburbs were already in Japanese hands, but the city centre was still unoccupied. In the distance, like fireworks and crackers exploding, like a mammoth bonfire night, the marines heard the sounds of gunfire. Aircraft swooped low over the dockyard, then soared up again into the sky. They were all Zero fighters; nothing bearing the familiar RAF roundel appeared.

There was something unreal about the whole scene, thought Doyle. He felt he was not part of it, but an onlooker; it was difficult to comprehend the horrible reality: that within hours they could be surrounded, the docks seized, with, at best, indefinite incarceration as prisoners facing them all.

An Indian, wearing the uniform of an officer in the Royal Indian Navy, white shoes, socks, shorts and shirt, came into the building and approached Major Johnston. He explained he had seen them come ashore from *Enterprise* and offered to help in any way the Major could suggest.

Johnston turned to his men.

'Gather round,' he told them. This officer here will be in charge of our three launches. He speaks Burmese perfectly, and he must be obeyed on all occasions when we are afloat. Not only may our lives depend on his decisions, but so will the success of our operation, which is more important. These launches appear all that is left of Burma's navy – at least around here. We will load them up, then take off to harry the enemy until reinforcements arrive. I am assured they are on the way.'

When the launches were ready, with drums of diesel and lubricating oil aboard, water tanks filled, the Major again called the men together.

'Get out and rummage about in any of the stores for any food you can find and bring it back here within half an hour. After that, we sail. No returning for any stragglers. Synchronize watches.'

Several marines discovered cases of beer, others bottles of whisky and gin. Wiser ones brought cans of food, biscuits, bags of rice.

'Why the haste, sir?' someone asked the Major.

'The engineers are blowing up all the warehouses and dock installations in exactly thirty-five minutes and we have to be away or risk going up with them. That's why.'

The marines climbed aboard the launches.

'Cast off,' ordered the Indian officer.

Each launch had a Burmese *sarang* in charge of the daily running of the craft. He steered her, standing in his *longyi*, hands on the wheel, a cheroot gripped firmly in his mouth. They moved up and into the middle of the river, dropped anchor, waited. Across the water they could see cars starting up in the dock buildings and racing for the gates. Men still came running out with whatever they could carry, a box of tools, a bottle of whisky. They also ran for the gates.

A whistle blew, and for a moment there was total silence. Then a black ball of smoke arose slowly, with a white-hot heart of flame. The sound of the explosions came a split second later. Cranes collapsed and rooftops. Buildings fell in. Doyle looked up and saw the air thick and dark with falling debris. He shouted a hoarse warning.

'Heads down!'

A huge block of concrete, big as a partners' desk, careered out of the sky and dropped two feet in front of their bows. Now one explosion followed another and the air turned grey and abrasive with concrete dust.

The wind fanned flames and carried the scorched smell of burning wood and paint.

The marines stared with a kind of fascinated horror at the scene; it might have been a spectacle specially staged for their enjoyment. It seemed impossible to accept that this vast and deliberate destruction could involve or affect them in any way whatsoever. Nor did they appreciate at once that this was the end of Rangoon. Until the wharves and docks had been destroyed, there always remained the hope, illusory perhaps – although the Major had believed it – that reinforcements would arrive. Indeed, only days earlier, the Seventh Hussars had sailed in with their tanks, unloaded at the docks and immediately set off up the road north into the heart of Burma to join the rearguard. But with neither docks nor dockyard workers, it would now be impossible to reinforce the retreating British and Indian armies.

Doyle was aboard *Rita*. He made his bed down on deck with the others and watched the fires on the docks burn themselves out. Within a few hours they had died down, with nothing more to consume, and the marines lay looking at the huge Burma moon and bright unfamiliar stars. The launches rocked gently at anchor as the tide turned. Apart from distant bursts of gunfire, the occasional peal of a whistle, or the blare of a car horn, the night seemed ominously silent. Very few lights burned now in Rangoon. The generating station was out of action; most of the lights the marines could see came from hurricane lamps or the torches of looters. It was difficult to believe that, only weeks before, this had been one of the great cities of the East.

Next morning the *sarangs* started up their engines and the launches crossed to a wooden jetty that had not been destroyed. The marines climbed ashore and went into the town. Their orders were to tell anyone and everyone they met that they were an advance guard of several thousand Australians who should be landing any day.

The Australian Infantry Division were actually at that moment sailing from the Middle East, had rounded the southern tip of India, and were on their way back to Australia to repel any Japanese invasion there. Mr Churchill had cabled to the Australian Prime Minister, Mr Curtin, to ask if he would agree to diverting this Division to Burma. He felt that its presence could conceivably prevent the loss of that country and a consequent break in communications with China. President Roosevelt agreed with Churchill, but Curtin would not be moved. He was determined that they should be in their homeland in case of a Japanese move south. The

Governor of Burma, Sir Reginald Dorman-Smith, cabled to the War Cabinet in London: 'It is of infinite importance to us to know whether Australian Division will arrive. Please say yes or no.'

The answer was the latter alternative. Churchill cabled back: 'We have made every appeal, reinforced by President, but Australian government absolutely refuses. Fight on.'

The marines, of course, did not know of this exchange of views and news, but even so, without proper docking facilities, their claim that Australians were coming lacked credibility, although they passed it on with what conviction they could.

As they moved through the city's streets, they began to appreciate the scale of chaos that prevailed. Every house that could be broken into, every shop deserted by its owner, had been ransacked. Goods of all kinds littered the pavements: refrigerators, radiograms, sofas, chairs too heavy to be carried away, even a grand piano. As a warning to other potential looters, whenever they found locals actively looting premises or carrying away goods obviously not their own, they beat them with rifle butts or bamboo canes. But they caught very few out of hundreds.

The Judicial Secretary in Rangoon, Mr Fielding Hall, had in his charge prisons, homes for mental patients, and leper asylums. The local staffs had fled and it was impossible to remove criminals or the ill and insane – often very violent cases – to the relative safety of North Burma. There were no vehicles to transport them, and the only road was already jammed with refugees. Trains had ceased to run and there were no boats capable of ferrying them up the Irrawaddy River. Equally, several thousand men and women could not be kept in prisons and hospitals without guards, food or care.

In these appalling circumstances he gave orders that they should all be released to fend for themselves as best they could with any friends or relatives. He believed that this was his duty, because otherwise they could literally starve to death, but their release added a bizarre quality to an already tragic situation. The streets of Rangoon were suddenly crowded with maniacs, murderers, rapists, who ran, shaven-headed, half-clad, carrying clubs, crow-bars, anything they could use to break down a frail door or smash through the window of a house. Lepers, their faces and bodies appallingly disfigured, eyes like cloudy giant marbles in their heads, also roamed the city, chanting or gibbering, drunk on bottles of neat whisky others had procured for them. And with them came lunatics, dancing, prancing, cavorting in the terrible private worlds of the insane.

Doyle and the other marines watched these crazy people skipping past, picking at debris on rubbish heaps, brandishing things they had found, a child's doll, a silk cushion, half a violin.

Some were pyromaniacs and crouched over fires they lit on pavements or under abandoned cars, in empty houses. Soon they had fires blazing in nearly every street. With the strength of madness, lunatics dragged doors, window frames and logs to pile on embers that would otherwise have died down. When the Judicial Secretary realized the extent of the damage they were causing, and the horror that the release of so many murderers and maniacs struck in the hearts of the few citizens remaining in the doomed city, he was overcome by revulsion at what he had done and took his own life.

Now a further hazard appeared: wild animals. Rangoon Zoo in pre-war times had been one of the finest in the East. But now, without keepers or wardens, the animals could not be kept in cages, uncared for, to die of hunger or thirst. The Zoo's senior staff lacked means to kill them humanely in the short time available, so they opened the locks of the cages and set them free to find what food they could.

Tigers, lions, hyenas, giraffes, elephants roamed streets already piled high with debris, and corpses no one could be found to bury. This situation brought hazards of its own. The Rev. Neville Metcalfe, chaplain to the Seventh Hussars, was about to sit down on the trunk of a fallen tree to rest in the heat, when suddenly he saw that the trunk had eyes and teeth and was watching him speculatively. He had nearly sat on the snout of an escaped alligator.

For Doyle and the members of Force Viper, however, one of the saddest and most poignant sights was to watch the packs of dogs that ran barking and wailing through the city. These were former household pets abandoned by their owners and now reverting to their wild state.

To Doyle, as to many others with him, there was a growing air of unreality about their role. To thrash a few looters and avoid criminals and madmen was not a contribution they felt they could best make. They sensed they were simply marking time, and all the while Japanese troops were steadily moving in from the outer suburbs. It could only be days, perhaps even only hours, before they reached the docks and the tank farm (as the area containing the great oil storage tanks was called) fell into their hands, with enough fuel to supply their vehicles and aircraft for months if not years.

The marines were leaving the three launches each morning and returning before nightfall to sleep aboard. On this particular evening, with launches moored side by side, Major Johnston addressed them all.

'The oil tanks are going to be blown up tomorrow,' he told them. 'We will stay in the area until the last moment, because the demolition parties have to get away. We will provide covering fire for their withdrawal.

'When the Japs see one tank go up in flames, they will use every effort to get into the farm and stop the others being destroyed. They have a very great initiative to do this – one hundred and fifty million gallons of petrol, aviation fuel, kerosene, in these tanks. Enough to keep them going all the way north into India – and then maybe link up with the Germans in the Middle East. It is our job to stop them.'

Oil company executives had actually made plans for this vast destruction even before the Japanese bombed Pearl Harbor and Singapore, but only to be implemented when there was no possible hope of saving them. The tank farm at Syriam was on an enormous scale and represented generations of work by British and Burmese. Each tank contained between one million and two million gallons of oil; they were spread over an area of three square miles. In addition, there was a further square mile of refineries with a powerhouse, workshop and offices.

The engineers due to carry out the task

had ten tons of gelignite at their disposal. The marines escorted them in commandeered cars to the tanks and helped them to unload the gelignite, which had been split up into roughly 700 explosive charges. Each of these weighed between 30 and 40 pounds, and they had to be placed around the oil tanks in locations chosen where they could inflict most damage.

Doyle and the others then crammed the cars with the records and other documents of the Burmah Oil Company and manhandled them on to barges to be towed upriver. Doyle's special task was to supervise the burning of all payrolls, and the personal files of every Burmese employee, so that the Japanese would not be able to trace them and force them to try and restart the refinery.

The actual command to set the tanks alight was delayed for as long as possible, because once they were burning the fires could not be stopped. Also, when they had started, locals for possibly a hundred miles around the flat country would see the great black mushrooming cloud of oil fumes, and sense that this was the funeral pyre for Burma under British rule.

The demolition was finally set for lunchtime on a Saturday. The marines and a detachment of Gurkhas dug protective trenches around the perimeter. Disregarding the time difference, Doyle wondered what they would be doing back in Middlesbrough at this hour. Would there be a football match? Would the pubs be full, and the market busy, with the stalls selling whatever they could find in wartime? Where would his friends be, his parents? Whatever they might be doing, they would never imagine how he was about to spend this particular Saturday afternoon.

At the blast of a whistle the marines and oilmen began to open the huge mastercocks on each storage tank. A black glutinous tide of oil streamed across the yards.

In the midday heat the petrol content evaporated quickly, and then a dangerous and explosive mixture hung in dark clouds just above the tops of the tanks. The marines and Gurkhas now climbed into their trenches and waited. No one was quite clear whether the explosion would blow upwards or outwards, and when it came they were all unprepared for the sight. One moment the silver-painted tanks stood like giant gas-holders, sharply silhouetted against the sky. Cranes in the dockyard pointed down towards them. The air trembled with petrol fumes and heat. The next moment there came a deep, almost subterranean rumble, followed by another, and another, and then dozens more as the charges detonated. The tanks now erupted in a gigantic blaze that dried the breath in the throats of the watchers.

Doyle saw a ball of fire, at least a mile wide, ascend into the sky, and then he ducked into his trench as fragments of metal and concrete rained down. Some of these weighed tons. Metal rods and pipes, white with heat, fell into the water that boiled around them. Other pieces of debris crashed through the roofs of huts and buildings. The roar of the explosion deafened him, punching all thought from his head.

The marines looked at each other in bewilderment, momentarily unable to absorb the magnitude of the destruction. Their next task was to set fire to the trucks and cars, for the transport jetties were jammed bonnet to tail with vehicles. Some were empty, others full of equipment and food, and all abandoned by their drivers. In addition, there were dozens of pack mules, now whinnying, stamping their hooves and tossing their heads in terror at the blaze. They could not be left to burn alive. The most humane way in the circumstances was also the quickest: they were sprayed with tommy-gun fire.

The sky grew dark with the heavy pall of smoke, and Doyle and others switched on the headlights of as many trucks as they could in order to see their way back to the launches.

As they ran through the blaze, they passed incongruous signs – 'No Smoking, Danger –

Fire Risk', and rows of red fire extinguishers still full, clipped to fire points around the walls. The heat burned the hairs off the back of Doyle's neck and his hands, making him choke and gasp for breath. He was astonished to see the faces of his colleagues had been blackened with flecks of oil – and then realized that he must look equally odd to them.

When they reached the launches, Major Johnston checked them all aboard: no casualties, no stragglers, no one left behind. The *sarangs* opened the throttles, eager to be away, and the launches took off upriver. Many of the tanks were on the river bank so that they could be discharged more easily into tankers. As a result, millions of gallons of fuel were polluting the river water – and ahead of them, as far as they could see, stretched flames burning on the water, ten, twenty, thirty feet high. The marines ducked their heads as the bows hit them, and the launches bucked and reared under full throttles through a wall of flame.

The men held their breath, lying flat on deck, covering their eyes with their hands to gain what protection they could against the heat. Then they were out through the flames, with bubbles of scorched and blistered paint on the launches. Behind them, half a hundred years of planning, exploration, drilling and building had gone up in flames within minutes in an inferno that was to burn day and night for the next six weeks.

The engineers and oil company executives in charge of the demolition, about a hundred strong, had made for a ship waiting offshore. This was to head south to the open sea to take them to Calcutta.

Doyle's task was to crouch in the bows of his launch with a tommy-gun, covering the withdrawal of the demolition party. The marines' next assignment was to go inshore again and transfer a number of RAF men to a British oil tanker standing in the river mouth. Scramble nets were already over the side of the tanker and the marines held their launches close to as the Air Force crews climbed up. When they were all aboard, some of the marines began to follow them. Their job was done; there was nothing left to blow up on the shore, and the Japanese must already be at the gates of the blazing refinery. Major Johnston ordered them back.

'Where the hell are you going?' he shouted. 'We've got a job to do.'

'I thought it had finished, sir,' cried someone.

'It hasn't bloody started!' he retorted.

They pushed off reluctantly from the tanker with boat-hooks.

'Where are we bound for then, sir?' someone asked.

'There's a canal here, the Twante Canal, that links up with the Irrawaddy. We're going upriver to deny every boat we see to the Japanese.'

This canal led from the mouth of Rangoon Bay into the Irrawaddy, and along this the three launches now went in convoy. Major Johnston travelled in the first with the Indian naval officer, Captain Alexander in the second, Lieutenant Cave in the third. The banks of the canal reached out to within feet of the blistered sides of the boats, and everyone was glad to be through and out into the main river.

Doyle remembered from geography lessons at St Patrick's that this was the most important river in Burma. It rose in the northeast of Assam near the Tibet frontier, and ran south for nearly fifteen hundred miles. At its mouth the river discharged through the delta into the Bay of Bengal. It was probably three miles wide at the point they entered, and although the end of the dry season was approaching, the current was still strong and swift.

In peacetime paddle steamers of the Irrawaddy Flotilla Company sailed regularly north from Rangoon to Mandalay and then back to Rangoon. Usually they anchored each evening off a town or village because hundreds of local passengers preferred these riverboats to the railway which ran alongside the river, and very few owned cars. The river brought down an immense amount of mud and so after every monsoon it was silted up on both sides. This meant that only a relatively narrow channel in the centre was deep enough for the larger vessels.

Huge stakes marked this navigable section for oil tankers and other boats that brought cargoes of teak or concrete down from a factory that had been established on the bank in the 1930s. A number of smaller craft also used the river, and immense rafts were a peculiarity of the Irrawaddy and its sister river, the Chindwin. These were so large, seemingly the size of floating tennis courts, that huts were built on each one and whole families lived aboard them.

At night the three launches anchored off the east bank, not in the mainstream, and equally not too close to land in case Japanese units had already marched north. The mainstream would be dangerous, and posed a hazard, because other craft moving up and down the river might not see them as they rode at anchor without lights.

Every morning Doyle and several other marines would go ashore and into the nearest village, usually with the *sarang* or one or other of the few Burmese who constituted the crew. Sometimes the Burmese headman would speak a little English and make himself understood, and would barter for chickens with cigarettes or cans of diesel oil. They would also find out from him whether there were any strangers in the area. The word 'stranger' was their synonym for Japanese or for a new hazard, men of the so-called Burmese National Army, who had thrown in their lot with the Japanese as being more likely to win the war than the retreating British.

After these forays ashore the three launches would sail out into mid-channel and stop each vessel passing up and down. If the boat was of a size likely to be of any use to the enemy, they would conduct it to the bank, put all passengers ashore and fire a tommy-gun burst into the hull below the waterline.

None of the marines relished this task, for they knew that these sampans and other craft carried the produce that local Burmese had to sell in order to survive. It was no way to win their friendship, or even their loyalty. The wretched owners went down on their knees, kissing their feet and legs, to try and persuade them to allow their particular boat to sail past. They would offer them their daughters, their wives, anything, if only they would agree, but the answer had always to be a regretful shake of the head and a burst of fire.

One morning the Indian naval officer accompanied Doyle and the Royal Marines patrol into a village larger than the rest. The headman admitted that three strange Indians had arrived late on the previous night.

'Where are they?' asked the naval officer.

We locked them up for the night. We did not trust them,' the headman replied.

'Bring them out.'

Three bedraggled Indians, with their hands tied with lengths of rope, were marched out of the primitive jailhouse, and an interrogation took place. The Indian officer explained to Major Johnston that on each of these men had been found grenades, revolvers, and a number of rounds. They were members of the pro-Japanese Indian National Army, which had been formed largely from Indian troops taken prisoner by the Japanese at the fall of Singapore. They admitted that they had arrived in the village in order to try and persuade the launches to come close to the bank and then sink them with their grenades.

The Indians were marched back to jail, and the patrol returned to the launch. The Indian naval officer conferred with Major Johnston, who sent for the other officers, including Lieutenant Cave. That afternoon Cave called everyone aboard *Rita* on deck.

'I want twelve volunteers for a nasty job,' he said. 'But one that has to be done. We drew lots and I drew the short straw.'

'What is it, sir?' asked Doyle.

'Firing squad,' came the brief reply.

Doyle wanted no part in this, but twelve men eventually volunteered and went ashore with the naval officer. The officer explained that as soon as the launches moved on, he believed that the Indians were almost certain to be freed, and having seen the launches at close quarters, they would be able to give the Japanese a good idea of their speed. It would therefore only be a matter of time – and probably very little time – before the Japanese would mount a much more professional attack.

The men had to be dealt with; it was a 'them or us' situation, and as such it had to be them. They were now brought out from the jail and the patrol marched them to the river bank. The whole village turned out to watch. At the officer's orders, the twelve marines raised their rifles.

'Firing squad,' he ordered, 'Single rounds, *fire!*'

Rifles cracked like circus whips, and birds flew screaming out of the trees with a great flurry of wings. The three men collapsed on the river bank. The villagers looked at them and then at the squad, who marched back aboard *Rita*. The *sarangs* started the engines and the three launches moved off upriver.

The locals stood in a silent cluster for a moment, and then walked back to their homes. Doyle could feel an almost physical wave of hostility emanate from them towards the marines. It was the same feeling he had experienced in the Maldives, after the graves had been uncovered, but much more intense, infinitely more dangerous.

The Indian naval officer came up to him, offered him a cigarette.

'A bad business,' he said. 'But we had to do it. The only thing I hope is that none of us ever fall into their hands. They'd give us the same treatment then – only not so swift and painless.'

The same thought had occurred to Doyle and to the other marines. That day there was little conversation aboard *Rita;* everyone was too concerned with his own thoughts.

Later, one man asked Doyle, 'Where's the officer?'

Doyle shrugged. He knew where he was, but did not want to admit what he knew. Lieutenant Cave had been so overcome at the order he had given, and had so hated giving, that since his return he had been vomiting over the side of the launch.

The marines had absolute trust in Major Johnston. To them he appeared almost middle-aged – he was no more than 30 – and they naively assumed that by reason of his age and rank he must have knowledge of reinforcements and plans that was denied to them. They did not realize that, although he was in radio contact with other British units, he knew little more than they did.

Aboard *Rita* was an old clockwork gramophone with a single record, Fats Waller playing 'My Very Good Friend, the Milkman'. To while away hours watching river banks, expecting a burst of enemy fire or the wham of a mortar shell at any moment, they played this record over and over again. When the needle grew blunt, they sharpened it on a whetstone. They only began to appreciate the strain under which the Major was living when, one day he suddenly picked up this gramophone and flung it, still playing the record, into the river. This action was quite out of character, and made them all realize that their position could be more serious than any of them had hitherto imagined, or even allowed themselves to consider.

Days passed as they sailed up and down the river, intercepting and sinking local craft. Time seemed to have lost all meaning; unease about their own predicament grew with every passing hour. The launches could carry only a limited supply of diesel, and what they could trade for food ashore was also dwindling. It was unsafe to drink untreated river water, and they had to boil cans of it and allow it to cool.

Food was running low and the Major gave the order for all three launches to sail north to the nearest large town, Prome. Here they anchored and went ashore. They could not see any signs of the Japanese and were able to fill the tanks with diesel and stock up with food from an army unit. More importantly, they met a remarkable character, Major Michael Calvert.

He had been born to India, the youngest of four brothers. While he was at school in England, his brothers joined the Royal Engineers, and Calvert decided to do the same. He won a place at the Royal Military Academy in Woolwich, later read Mechanical Science at Cambridge, where he was awarded a half blue for swimming and water polo, and also boxed for the university and, later, for the army.

Calvert served in Hong Kong and Shanghai, but when war broke out he was back in England and took part in the abortive Norway landing. After a spell in a special commando unit in Scotland, he was sent to Australia to establish a commando school there. From Australia Calvert was posted to Maymyo, Burma's summer capital, north of Mandalay.

Here, in what was known as the Bush Warfare School, he instructed British and Australian officers and NCOs in the rudiments of guerrilla fighting before they were posted to help the Chinese in their war with Japan. Americans maintained an air warfare mission in Burma, training pilots for a similar purpose.

The object in the British case was to occupy the Japanese Army with the Chinese, in the slender hope that, although a member of the Axis, Japan might not attack British possessions in the East.

Calvert equipped his men with Australian bush hats which were infinitely more suitable for jungle warfare than the solar topis issued to British troops serving in Burma, whose khaki drill shorts and bush jackets were also a relic of peacetime soldiering before the First World War. They wore leather boots and grey socks, over which they had to pull curious woollen tops like khaki leg warmers, known as hosetops.

This dress was useless in jungle conditions. Calvert kitted out his group, known as 'Calvert's Commandos', with green uniforms of thin drill cloth. His men included Australians, Scots from the Royal Scots and the Gordon Highlanders, and other soldiers from the Middlesex Regiment, the Leicesters, East Surreys and Loyals. Many had criminal records, either as soldiers or civilians, or both. All were hard, tough and relished a fight. Calvert needed reinforcements, because the more men he had, the more he could achieve; Royal Marines were therefore very welcome.

Major Johnston explained to him that Force Viper's original orders had been to patrol the east coast of the Gulf of

Martaban in whatever craft they could find to prevent the Japanese from coming behind the British troops and cutting off their retreat. They arrived too late to attempt this, and since no further orders had reached them, they had worked on their own initiative, destroying all craft he thought could have any potential value to the enemy.

Calvert's brief was to safeguard the west bank of the river. He considered that the best way to carry this out was to concentrate on the main town on that bank, Henzada, a township about the size of Eastbourne, and for which the Japanese would be bound to aim. At his command he had a paddle steamer from the Irrawaddy Flotilla Company, *Hastings*. This was a large vessel, 300 feet long and about 40 feet wide. Because of the sandbanks and silting of the river, she had been built with a draught of about three feet and looked rather like a Mississippi riverboat. This vessel had just arrived in Prome carrying hundreds of refugees from Rangoon. Now, with his group aboard and as many explosives as he could find, and with the marines coming behind, they headed south in convoy.

Whenever Calvert saw a potential target, he engaged it on the premise that, since he might pass that way but once, so anything he could do it would be well to do then, since he might not pass that way again. His men went ashore to blow up trucks, to mine the railway line, and sink any large boat, barge or sampan anchored along the river bank. The *Hastings* would stay out in mid-river while *Rita* drew closer to the shore. The Indian naval officer would strip off his uniform, put on the white shirt and dhoti Indians generally wore, and Doyle, with another marine, would row him across to the bank. He would then vanish into the trees.

On this particular evening Doyle thankfully rowed back to *Rita* and waited, watching for a signal, which he would make after dark: three short flashes and one long, from a torch. The night was hot and filled with deceptively peaceful sounds of laughter, the clatter of aluminium pans on cooking fires, a dog barking, someone singing in an unknown tongue. Gradually the night became alive with unnumbered specks of glowing light that surged and died and surged again – fireflies going through their elaborate courtship. The female took up a position and flashed the tiny light that attracted the male and also guided him to her as he literally flew on the beam.

Doyle waited as patiently as he could, envying the fireflies their rites of love, and becoming increasingly uneasy at the length of time the Indian officer was remaining ashore. A dozen explanations presented themselves, each one more sinister than the one preceding it. Then, at last, he saw the brief, pale flicker of the torch. Thankfully, he climbed down into the rowing boat and rowed ashore as silently as he could to bring him back.

With each dip of the oars he paused, back arched, as though by bracing his muscles he could deflect a bullet, but there was nothing. Even the sounds of life ashore had diminished; it was difficult to believe that a large town could be beyond the thick belt of trees. He could not see any lights; the trees might conceal a city not of the living, but of the dead.

The Indian officer reported that he had not seen any Japanese in Henzada; everything appeared peaceful and normal. Many people must have left to travel north, taking with them all the cars and trucks they could find. This would account for the quietness, which he found extraordinary after their time in Rangoon.

Calvert and Johnston now agreed their plan of action. At eight o'clock on the following morning the marines would land with Calvert's commandos, who would blow up the oil tanks. The marines would provide a back-up force in case the Japanese arrived during the night, and in addition would help to cover their withdrawal.

But at eight o'clock, when everyone was ready to leave, an unexpected mist, 10 feet high, lay on the surface of the river. This was so thick that they could not see the bank. They waited, cursing the mist, each man working out his own mental calculation as to whether this and the resulting delay were harmful or beneficial to their chances of survival.

By noon the mist had cleared. *Rita* picked up the commandos from the paddle steamer, and more marines from the other launches, and ferried them as close to the banks as they could reach. Thick reeds and mud brought a strong risk of fouling their propeller, so everyone went over the side into the water, some to wait on the bank, others, under Major Calvert, to go forward. The bank was unusually high, built to protect the low-lying land behind it from flooding during the flood-tide monsoon.

From the bank, what they could see of Henzada did not impress them. There was a square, with stone or brick buildings around it, then a long area of wooden buildings, like English barns, some built up on wooden stilts. Crowds of locals had appeared from these buildings, and gathered around the new arrivals. Some wanted to shake hands with them; they all appeared friendly, smoking cheroots, grinning cheerfully. Doyle was reminded of a visiting amateur football team being made welcome by the home side for a friendly match.

Calvert had brought with him a Burmese engineer from the paddle steamer. Now this man acted as his interpreter. Pointing to the bush hat he was wearing, Calvert explained that he was leading an advance party of thousands of Australian troops, who would help to rid Burma of the hated Japanese invaders. This announcement brought cheers and handclaps from the crowd. Everyone seemed to be smiling. Old men with wrinkled faces puffed happily at their cheroots, young men in *longyis* stood, arms folded, nodding their heads cheerfully in approval.

'In fact,' Calvert went on, warming to his own oratory in view of this reaction, 'I can tell you that the whole of Burma will be liberated in a matter of days.'

As the interpreter began to translate this, a man behind the crowd called in English: 'Lay down your arms! You are surrounded!'

Instantly Calvert swung his tommy-gun in the direction of the speaker. Was this a hoax, someone's foolish idea of a joke? He waited. For a moment, no one spoke, no one moved. Then he saw movement behind the crowd, which parted to let some men come through. They were oddly dressed in cast-off pieces of uniform, belts, packs, Japanese or British caps. Others wore the traditional *longyis*. All held machine-guns. Calvert guessed correctly that they were members of the Burma National Army who, like the

Indian prisoners of war, had elected to fight on the side of the Japanese. He was so surprised, his voice dried up completely. He moved his lips but no sound came. One of his corporals was not so afflicted.

'*Bollocks!*' he bellowed, and fired his tommy-gun magazine into the armed men.

Instantly there was uproar. Dead and dying fell to the ground with a clatter of arms. The crowd scattered, screaming in horror and surprise. This was not how they had imagined the confrontation would be. Hogs, dogs, cows were caught in the shambles, as people fought to escape another burst of fire. Now at the far side of the square, a large contingent of Japanese troops appeared at the double.

Doyle and the other marines, lying flat on the ground with the river behind them and the bank blocking their view, heard the chatter of guns but could see nothing. Now, on the top of the bank a Burmese Buddhist priest, a *pongyi*, with shaven head and wearing saffron robes, stood up against the sky.

The Burmese, Doyle knew, were Buddhists, and every Burmese man was supposed to spend a certain time as a *pongyi* or monk. These monks were more than religious mentors; they were virtually the schoolmasters of the country, and carried out this task in return for alms from the people they taught. Their influence was therefore considerable, spiritually and morally.

This *pongyi* waved cheerfully to the marines, pointing behind him. He seemed to be waving a welcome or inviting them to come on up and over the bank. The marines needed no further encouragement. They started to run up the bank, and at that moment a Japanese officer appeared next to the *pongyi*, sword in hand.

'Drop your arms!' he shouted in English. 'You are surrounded by machine-guns!'

The marine next to Doyle raised his rifle and picked off the officer with a single shot. Then he swung his rifle to the right and shot the *pongyi*.

Major Calvert and his men now fell back from Henzada and ran down the bank, with the marines giving covering fire as they waded out to the launches. Hardly were they all aboard than more Japanese arrived with mortars, and began to shell them. The paddle steamer had machine-guns mounted behind sandbags along her decks. These now opened up on the Japanese on shore, firing tracer bullets, one in every five, so they could see where they landed. The shells set fire to trees and grass, and behind, near the town, the oil tanks were blazing with the now familiar black smoke casting a shroud over the brilliant hearts of flame.

The *Hastings* now went back to Prome to deposit the wounded, refuel and take on more ammunition. The marines had left several dead on the river bank, and with the wounded taken off in the paddle steamer, their absence aboard the launches was most marked. Where they had been packed tight on the decks, now there was plenty of space, but all would much rather have been crowded together, because those who had left would not be returning; and with them had gone something of the spirit of Force Viper, in the sense of experiences shared for many months.

They sailed south, and now Japanese units, hidden on the banks in the thick trees, began to fire mortars at them. The *sarangs* swung the launches to port, to starboard, to port again, to avoid the bursting shells that exploded harmlessly in the brown river water. Doyle was thrown a smoke canister and told to make smoke and so give the launches some cover. The canister was of an old-fashioned type, with a pliable strip of metal at one end covering a small hole. This strip had to be bent back and forwards against the tin, and it would then break off to release the smoke through the hole.

He raced forward with this, flinging himself flat on the deck. Bullets from machine-guns on the shore were now pinging off the armour plate or thudding into the sandbags. He seized the tin strip and wrenched it furiously. Nothing. He could hear anguished shouts from the stern of the launch: 'Doyle! Make smoke, *make smoke!*'

The strip of metal came away uselessly in his hand. The canister was a dud.

Just then a great cloud of black smoke erupted from *Doris* and the wind obligingly blew it over all three launches. The firing stopped momentarily. Doyle threw the useless canister into the river.

Half a mile from the blazing buildings Doyle suddenly noticed a man waving frantically to them from the bank. He was wearing a khaki Army shirt and shorts but had no hat. He waved a piece of rag and it was clear that every movement of his arm was an agony to him. *Rita* turned in towards the bank. The man saw them and, as though the effort of standing had become too much, he sank down on his hands and knees. He was obviously too weak to swim, so two marines waded ashore and carried him out to the launch.

They laid him down on his back on the deck. He was in great pain and motioned feebly towards his stomach. When they lifted his shirt, they saw that he had suffered half a dozen bayonet thrusts in his groin.

Weakly, he explained how he had received them. He was one of Major Calvert's commandos left behind unconscious and thought to be dead. After the brief bloody battle, the Japanese dragged all wounded men to a hut and bolted the door from the outside. For twenty-four hours the wounded lay there, in an extremity of pain, without food, water or any sanitation, with the only dressing for their wounds the little field dressing pads of gauze and bandage they carried in their trouser pockets.

Then the Japanese major who had commanded the attack opened the door. He explained in English to the wounded men, some by now comatose from their injuries, others delirious with fever and festering open wounds, that he had just received a draft of twenty young soldiers. They had not yet taken part in any battle. Their only bayonet practice had been on straw dummies. Now they were going to be blooded in a different way.

The wounded men were pulled out of the hut. Many were too weak to walk, some too badly wounded even to stand. The Japanese soldiers bound them to palm trees with jungle creeper and rope. The young soldiers fixed bayonets and faced their wounded enemies. At the major's command, they charged at their living targets: in, out, on guard, follow through. Most of the prisoners took several bayonet thrusts in their chests, stomachs and groins before they died in fearful agony. The man who told the story had lost consciousness and came round to find himself lying under the bodies of his friends. They had been cut down after the bayoneting. He lay beneath the dead and the dying until the Japanese moved away and then, slowly and painfully, he had crawled to the river bank.

It was clear that he would not live for more than a few hours: in addition to his original wounds, he had severe internal bleeding. He died later that night, but before he did so he managed to whisper the general location of the main Japanese camp, several miles downstream.

This would be the next target for the launches.

They sailed on until Major Johnston gave the order to the *sarang* in the leading launch: 'Stop here.'

All *sarangs* throttled back their engines and threw their gears into reverse, just keeping enough power to withstand the downward current of the river. Johnston pointed towards the roofs of several wooden buildings just visible above the tops of the trees.

'Everything you've got into those buildings,' he ordered. 'Leave them something to remember us by.'

The Vickers guns stuttered away; the Bren guns lashed on the handrails barked; men with rifles crouched down, firing into the trees. Hot spent shell cases poured back inboard, scorching their bare legs, burning paint off the wooden decks.

Finally Johnston gave the command, 'Cease fire.' By then the buildings were blazing, tongues of flame pushed up and through the bamboo roofs. The marines could hear screams and shouts above the spasmodic firing of rifles, the crackle and roar of fiercely burning timber.

Turn the boats about,' ordered Johnston.

They sailed back upriver. On their way north they pulled in to reconnoitre a large village. Doyle, with half a dozen marines, went ashore as escort to the Indian naval officer, who again changed into local dress for his task. They waited on the perimeter of the village while he went ahead on his own. Later he returned. He reported that Japanese troops were approaching on the east bank, where there was a 'tank farm'. Plans had been made to destroy this, and so the Japanese advance must be delayed long enough for this delicate task to be carried out.

The party returned to the launches and when it grew dark the marines went ashore for a second time.

The plan was to ambush the Japanese on the only road, which followed the course of the river. Japanese soldiers wore boots with rubber soles, and so could march silently even on a metalled road. The marines wore issue boots with leather soles and metal studs, and therefore walked section by section on either side of the road in the thick sandy dust to minimize the sound of their approach.

The night was hot and humid. A pre-monsoon evening wind blew dust through their shirts, into the tops of their boots. The dust sandpapered their flesh against the weight of packs, water bottles, Bren gun magazines, grenades, and clips of ammunition in their pouches, as they trudged along.

The moon moved slowly up the sky, now glowing with an intensity never noticed in northern climates, now filtered by a lattice of branches and thick leaves. As they marched, they heard the croak of bullfrogs and the tuctoo, tuctoo of the lizard that took its name from the noise it made, a lizard always heard, rarely seen. These noises ceased as they approached, began again when they had passed.

It was possible for anyone familiar with the sounds of the jungle after dark to gauge the position of a stranger – much as a countryman can tell whether someone is approaching a field of horses or cattle, because momentarily they cease to eat and look towards the intruder. Doyle hoped that the Japanese were not able to decode these jungle signals of their approach.

He tried to keep his mind off the gloomier side of this possibility. If they were killed, that was one thing. But if they were wounded and captured, if they were left behind in the darkness, would they also end up, backs against palm trees, while sharpened bayonet blades were dug and turned and twisted in their guts? This was the uncomfortable reality. The Japanese army did not accept that prisoners had any rights: by allowing themselves to be captured they had forfeited all claims to live. They abided by this code themselves, and expected others to do the same. Many armies could talk of fighting to the last round and the last man: the Japanese actually did so.

As Doyle marched, head down, he noticed things he had never observed before, as though seeing for the first time that the eyelets in his boots, where the dubbined leather laces threaded through, were worn to smooth and polished metal; the laces had rubbed away all the black paint.

He could see the neck of the man in front of him, streaky with sweat and dust and scarred by some childhood operation or lanced boil, and he wondered what it had been. He was surprised he had never noticed this before, and in thinking when this might have occurred, Doyle thought back to his own childhood. Little incidents long forgotten now came up like twigs surfacing in the turmoil of a whirlpool.

He remembered street markets with pyramids of polished apples and pears, glowing under the hissing flare of naphtha lights. The arrival of a fair on waste ground; the crackle of a motorcycle engine on the wall of death; the swing and surge and rise and fall of merry-go-rounds and the pounding of the steam organ, with its little marionette figures mechanically strutting in and out, banging with their hammers.

He remembered his mother tucking him up in bed, and then listening to her footsteps going downstairs; the third step from the top always creaked. Then he and his brother would watch the shadows the street lamp outside made on the ceiling as the breeze moved the curtains of their window. Marching now, soaked in sweat, with the dull foreboding of imminent action heavy as a stone in his stomach, these homely simple images had an attraction he had never previously appreciated. He thought of days that had gone and would not come again; of friends who had gone with them since he had left Plymouth.

Suddenly he noticed that the section commander had held up his hand: images of the past vanished like a mist procession. All that was then; this was now.

They stopped, listening. The corporal motioned to them to take up positions farther away from the side of the road. In the distance, growing nearer, he could hear the faint clatter of accoutrements, the clop-clop of mules' hooves, muffled by dust. The Japanese soldiers could march on rubber soles: their mules still walked on iron shoes. They lay flat, slipped magazines on to the Bren guns, checked that the tommy-gun actuator handles were back, levers set for automatic fire. The moon rose above the trees and, as if on cue, with an almost theatrical timing, around the bend in the road, thirty yards ahead, came a company of Japanese. They were marching in single file. Doyle could see the mules and their packs, and the glitter of the moon on metal buckles and bayonet blades. They waited, watching, holding their fire, and as they waited, they saw with horror that this was not a patrol like theirs, not even fifty men, but hundreds, the leading company of a battalion on the march. Lieutenant Cave waited until the nearest were barely ten yards away, then shouted: *'Fire!'*

The night exploded with a crackle of automatic fire. Knife blades of flame flickered in the bushes. The leading Japanese dropped to the ground as soon as the firing started, some wounded, some dead, but the majority simply responding in the infantryman's only way to offer the smallest possible target. The mules took off, with a great neighing and bucking. Then, out of sight, came the boom-boom of mortars. A shell exploded feet from the marines. Chunks of tarmac and shrapnel rained down on them.

Doyle fired three magazines from his tommy-gun and then paused. His right boot suddenly felt damp as though he had trodden in warm water. He could not understand this and bent down to feel what had happened. The leather of the boot had been ripped through by a jagged piece of shrapnel. So had his gaiter. His fingers came away sticky, as though dipped in treacle. In the moonlight he saw it was blood, his blood.

At that moment he heard the order, 'Back to the boats! Get back!'

Marines were standing up now and running, stopping now and then to turn and fire towards the Japanese. The Japanese poured round after round into the group. More mortar shells landed with a blaze of phosphorus and roasting metal. Branches of trees crashed down on the road in flames. Men were dropping and rising and running and falling; it was difficult to know who was wounded or who had been tripped by a pothole or a broken branch. Doyle saw the glint of metal in the moonlight, the snout of a Bren gun poking through some bushes on his left, and an arm waving. He shouted, 'Get up and run.'

A voice shouted back in agony and terror, 'I can't! It's my leg! They've got me!'

A roar of another mortar bomb, a blaze of

light, a huge inverted cone of dirt that blotted out the moon and then no gun, no arm, nothing. He went on running. Ahead of him, someone doubled up suddenly and fell, tripping over his own rifle. A second leapt in the air as though on a spring and dropped in a mass of slings from his pack, his water bottle, his bandoliers. A third laid down his rifle cautiously on the road, and then, holding one hand to his stomach, sank down slowly, like an actor pretending to die in an amateur play.

Doyle went on running, came to a gap in the trees and climbed down from the bank into the warm lapping water. Both ankles felt sore, as though he had scratched them on brambles. He had done that often enough as a boy blackberrying in the woods outside Middlesbrough and paid no attention. He started to swim towards *Rita,* grateful for the refreshing coolness of the river. On either side other men were also swimming, choking, spitting out water, moving slowly, holding rifles or tommy-guns with one hand out of the river, threshing with their feet, the packs on their backs sticking up like rhinoceros humps.

Doyle reached *Rita.* Her engines were already running, exhausts bubbling. He climbed up the side, and then collapsed, exhausted, on the deck.

The *sarang* opened the throttle and *Rita*

turned out into mid-channel. The arrangement after any action ashore was always that the launches would wait in the area for two days in case any stragglers returned or any wounded managed to reach the river bank and signal to them.

They had to move up and down, however, because they were an obvious target for Japanese mortars, and shells fell all around them. Casualties had been high, ten men from *Rita* alone, with more from the other two launches. There was plenty of room now to lie on deck, plenty of room to dismantle the Bren guns and clean and oil them and replace them back behind the metal shields they had fixed in Rangoon, and the sandbags that were now leaking sand and dust. They waited for two days but no one else returned.

On reaching the launch Doyle had removed his boots and examined his ankles. The shrapnel had cut through his right leg to the bone; the wound gaped with a raw, red mouth. The cut on his left ankle was also deep, but not so serious; it might heal without stitches, but his right leg certainly needed a number of stitches.

This sort of treatment was quite impossible aboard the launch; there was not even any antiseptic left. All the medical officer could do was to bandage up both ankles as tightly as possible in the hope that the edges of the wounds would eventually grow together. This meant that Doyle could no longer lace up his boots, but this was no particular hardship since the Major explained that they were returning to Prome. It seemed unlikely that the Japanese had reached there yet, and they could put the wounded ashore for treatment, fill their fuel tanks with diesel and stock up with more rations.

On the third morning the sun seemed peculiarly bright, turning the usually oily and muddy surface of the water into a river of liquid gold. Doyle had never seen the sun shine so brilliantly, or the river appear so strange, so sinister in a way he could not describe. Suddenly the launch heeled sharply to starboard. The *sarang* was spinning the wheel frantically and shouting almost hysterically over his shoulder to the *sarangs* in the other two launches.

The second one followed, opening his throttles, so that the water churned into a great foaming wake. Doyle was astonished to see that both launches were heading straight for the river bank at full speed. Doyle braced himself as their bows cut into the mud and dug in for a distance of three or four feet. The *sarang* switched off his engines and the launch rocked and groaned, creaking in its unnatural position half afloat, half grounded.

Behind them the second launch was

executing the same manoeuvre. It was probably fifty yards away, when the sun simply went out, as suddenly as if someone had thrown a switch. One moment Doyle had been wondering at its unusual brightness, and then, as though he had been staring along the beam of a searchlight, it disappeared.

The sky was black, so that he could not see either of the other two launches. He could hear the roar of engines, and then a sudden silence as the *sarang* of the second launch switched off his engine.

Through the darkness he heard cries and screams and shouts for help. As his eyes grew accustomed to the gloom, he could see that the third launch had also turned, but too late. A giant tidal wave roaring up the river behind them had tipped it over, as though it was a child's toy. He saw the green under-hull, propeller still turning in the air, spraying beads of water, and then the launch was upside down, like a giant stranded sea beast.

All around it Doyle could see men bobbing in the river, frantically trying to grip any part of the boat, or holding up their hands, shouting for help. The huge wave carried them on and out of sight. Two men managed to reach the shore. Another couple swam against the current to *Rita*. Marines, leaning over the side, gripped them by their hands, but such was the force and fury of the torrent that they had to let go. They watched them being carried away, still waving and crying out for help that no one had the power to give.

The roar of the water and the noise of a wind that now swept through the trees, cracking trunks that did not bend, rose to a crescendo and then died as suddenly as it had begun. Within minutes the sun was shining again and the river had calmed, and what had happened might never have happened at all. The upturned launch, now at the centre of a rainbow-coloured oil patch, and the fact that possibly as many as twenty marines had drowned, provided grim evidence that it had. The *sarangs* aboard *Rita* and *Doris* started their engines and reversed out into the mainstream.

Such sudden storms frequently occurred on the Irrawaddy, the Indian naval officer explained. The only way to survive them was to put into shore immediately. To delay for minutes could be too late – as it had been too late for *Stella*. The two remaining launches chugged on slowly, the marines aboard them pondering the realization that, in addition to an enemy on land and enemy aircraft in the sky, they also had to fight the elements.

In case another similar storm struck them suddenly, they resolved to be better prepared. The launches carried several life-rafts lashed to the deck. Marines now untied the holding ropes and tied spare Bren guns, rifles and magazines to them so that if they had to take to the rafts, at least they would not go unarmed. They had to come in closer to the bank now, because the great wave appeared to have silted up the central navigational channel and they could not risk running aground and so presenting a static target.

On the road alongside the river they saw streams of refugees going north. There were a few motor cars, trucks and motorcycles, but most vehicles had been abandoned many miles south when they ran out of petrol. A few refugees had bicycles, but the rough roads and the heat had punctured tyres long ago and the cyclists rode on bare wheel rims, or pushed machines festooned with baggage of all kinds. Most refugees were walking, pushing handcarts or barrows with their belongings. Others carried their baggage on their backs. There were mothers with children sitting afork their thighs, men bearing enormous loads supported by straps and bands around their heads like coolies.

The marines were shocked at the sad and humiliating sight of British and Indian troops, many unarmed, wearing soiled and tattered shirts and shorts. Doyle could not dignify their shambling and defeated pro-gress by describing it as marching. These men were so demoralized that they did not even look up when they saw the launches running parallel to them upriver. They seemed beyond any sort of concentration, apart from simply keeping alive and on the road. North lay Assam and India and the prospect of safety, however illusory that hope might really be.

Casualties had been so heavy in Force Viper that not enough marines remained to man two launches, so the two boats stopped side by side in the centre of the river. Everyone transferred to *Rita* with fuel, weapons, ammunition and rations. The rear party opened the bilge cocks on the abandoned launch and watched it settle slowly in the swirling water. The radio, which until then had been working intermittently, now stopped. Major Johnston called all marines on deck – and the fact that all had space to fall in showed how Force Viper had been decimated.

'It's impossible to find out what's happening anywhere from now on, except by patrols ashore,' he said. 'The Rangoon area, as you know, is in Japanese hands. My last information on the radio was that they were advancing steadily up through the country. First, let us look at the bad news. It may be that their patrols are already north of this area. If not, they soon will be. We may use up all our fuel and ammunition and have to abandon ship. Or we may take a direct hit that sinks us.

'That's the bad news, and there's enough of it. Now for the good news. We are all Royal Marines – Plymouth marines. Our motto is *Per Mare, Per Terrain* – by sea, by land – so whether we are on the water or on the shore should be immaterial to us.

'Next, we are still a fighting force and our orders are to harry the enemy at every point – and we can and we will. And eventually, maybe not this week, or not even this year, but in the end, *we will win*. That's the best news of all.

'Your duty, if we go ashore and get split up, is to make your way back to headquarters, get yourself kitted out and back into the fight. No one wins a war by running away.'

He paused and eyed each marine in turn.

Where's headquarters, sir?' asked Doyle.

'You're all Plymouth marines,' Johnston replied. 'You know your headquarters. *Plymouth!*'

Downriver came a paddle steamer with a red cross painted on each side of her hull. The Japanese did not recognize Red Cross markings, but at that time this was not realized. As the steamer came within hailing distance, the medical officer ordered the launch alongside. The paddle steamer stopped with a great churning of reversed paddle blades. Half a dozen seriously wounded men, with arms blown off, and deep wounds in their stomachs and groins, were lifted aboard. With no medicines aboard the launch, the MO could do little for them except bind them with bandages that had already been used and washed over the side in the river, wrung out and used again and again.

Doyle's wounds had grown more and more painful, and their inflammation so great as the wounds suppurated, that he had spent much of his time on the deck with his feet dangling in the water in an attempt to ease the pain. This was growing worse. His feet had swollen up so that it was impossible to pull on a sock, let alone a boot, and now the doctor ordered him to leave aboard the paddle steamer.

'I'd rather stay,' Doyle told him. 'I started out with these blokes in Plymouth, and I want to go on with them.'

'You can't march with those ankles,' the medical officer replied. 'You can't walk a step without help. I'm sorry, but for all our sakes you've got to go. If we have to abandon ship, all we could do then would be to leave you with a rifle and one round. If you get on the hospital boat, there should be *some* treatment for you. I won't say there's much, but anything is an improvement on what we can give you here, which is virtually nothing.'

'Is that an order, sir?' asked Doyle.

'I'm sorry to say it is,' said the MO. 'And good luck. Maybe we'll meet again. I hope so. And in happier circumstances.'

'I hope so, too, sir,' said Doyle fervently. It seemed difficult to imagine circumstances less happy than their present situation.

Although despondent at the prospect of leaving men with whom he had already endured so much, Doyle realized the bitter truth of what the doctor said. He was a liability until he could have his wounds treated, and the remnants of Force Viper had no place for non-combatants. His ankles were so painful that they could not bear the weight of his body. He had to haul himself up the scramble-net on the side of the paddle steamer by his hands.

The wounded lay on deck; civilians, men of the Indian Army, the Royal Indian Navy, British and Australian soldiers. There were Indian traders, women with babies and children, families who had fled their homes and fallen ill on the way north. Every inch of deck space was filled.

An MO examined Doyle's feet, shook his head.

'What's the matter, sir?' asked Doyle in alarm at the look on the doctor's face.

'I'm not thinking about your legs so much,' replied the MO wearily. 'Given time – and drugs – we can cure them. But we haven't much of either. I'm thinking about your future. There is no point in beating about the bush. We'll almost certainly all be taken prisoner. The Japs are everywhere, up to the suburbs of Mandalay. And you won't get any medical treatment if they get hold of you. In fact, if they stay true to form, you won't need any.'

After the MO had passed on to his next patient, Doyle lay on deck, pondering what he had said. His orders from Major Johnston were to make for headquarters – wherever that might be – join up with other marines and carry the fight to the enemy. There could be no victory in retreat, in running away. But how could he find headquarters when he could not even walk?

Every so often, when a sampan was sighted moored near the bank, the ship slowed and then stopped. These sampans bobbed offshore, covered with screens of branches and leaves, looking like huge bushes in the water. Fitter patients climbed down the scramble-nets or gangway and approached them warily in case of an ambush. But the sampans only contained British or Indian troops, either delirious with fever, terribly wounded or dead. Some they could rescue, most they had to leave behind.

No weapons could be carried under the sign of the Red Cross, and if any of the staff found a rifle or a revolver concealed in a kitbag or dismantled in a pack, they immediately threw it into the river. Everything else that could be jettisoned was also thrown in the river to make more room for the wounded. On several occasions the Japanese could be seen standing on the shore watching them. Twice they machine-gunned the hospital ship. Two Indians were killed and several wounded.

The hospital ship now ceased its forays downriver; they were too dangerous to continue, and there was no further space for more passengers. They turned north now, and the farther north they went, the more bodies floated downriver past them.

Patients would wager half a cigarette to a whole cigarette whether a body floating in the river was that of a man or a woman. Mostly the men floated on their backs, and the women face down. Carcases of dogs, hogs, cows, all floated past, a sobering sight because the only water available to drink and bathe wounds was drawn up in a bucket from the river. Some was boiled in an old oil drum set up on the after deck, but this was a slow process and required wood to be gathered on shore patrols, so most water went untreated.

Doyle's wounds were now septic. He felt waves of fever grip his body; at one moment his skin would feel tight and taut and dry, and the next he would be soaked in a foul-smelling sweat. He was not certain whether he was delirious, but he knew his temperature was unusually high. He would sit in the shade of a cabin wall, remembering times past in Middlesbrough, in the Maldives, anywhere, and become confused with the rush of memories. Where was he? *Who* was he?

On the deck, close to him, two wooden tables from the saloon had been brought up and placed close together. On them, wounded in need of an operation were laid, for the two surgeons aboard to operate as best they could. They had no proper anaesthetic, just a pad of gauze soaked in chloroform or ether, that an orderly pressed over each patient's nose and mouth, with the order to breathe out. This was easier than asking them to breathe in, for some abhorred the smell of the chloroform. But if they emptied their lungs, they had to fill them again – and the only way to breathe in was through the filter of the gauze. The surgeons picked bullets out of bodies, amputated arms, legs, hands, fingers. Blood dripped off the tables on to the deck as they worked. Patients who were able hauled up buckets on ropes from the river and sluiced this blood away across the deck into the gunwales.

Next to Doyle on deck lay a young soldier, groaning in a kind of fevered stupor. When he could speak, he gasped at the pain in his stomach. The flesh was hot and dry. Doyle, touching it, was reminded of a time in the kitchen at Middlesbrough when he had accidentally held his hand over a gas burner on the kitchen stove.

There seemed no treatment for the man and no drugs. Doyle would dip a mug on a string down into the river and then pour the water he pulled up over his distended stomach in an attempt to ease his pain. Next morning Doyle woke up early and saw that someone had pulled a blanket across the soldier's face; he had died during the night. When they next stopped, two soldiers carried the body ashore, wrapped in his blanket, and buried him on the river bank.

A Chinese soldier, picked up somewhere north of Prome, had been shot in the chest with a string of bullets. It was amazing that, with such wounds, he still lived, for the doctors had no painkilling drugs and the bullets were buried too deeply in his body for them to remove with the few simple instruments at their disposal. The man lay gasping, each breath bubbling with blood, sobbing in his agony.

One morning, as the sun came up, he suddenly jumped to his feet and leapt over the side of the vessel into the flailing paddle wheel. Doyle hobbled to the rail, and could see the paddles going over him, splitting him. The water ran red with blood, and then he was gone in a pink-tinged wake.

The hospital ship put into Mandalay. The hope was that the worst of the ill and wounded could be transferred to a hospital, but this was not possible. An American officer stood on the quay. He had a pearl-handled revolver in his belt, and a number of Chinese soldiers with tommy-guns surrounded him. He seemed incongruous, like a figure out of some film. What was his purpose? What were his duties? Why was he there? Doyle never discovered, but he heard what the officer had to say.

'Mandalay's about to fall,' he told them grimly. 'Then it will be every man for himself. Everyone who can get out has already done so. If you offload your sick and wounded here, they will all be killed when the Japs come in. Your only hope is to head as far north as you can. And the farther you go, the better chance you give them – and yourselves.'

The captain of the hospital ship took the officer's advice. Drugs aboard had long since been exhausted. The patients now had only their natural physical resistance to help them recover, and this had already been grossly overstretched.

Food was low, and every morning brought new deaths. One afternoon the ship pulled into the shore to pick up several sick and wounded, although what good they could do for them was problematic. At least – or at most – they could transfer them a few more miles north. Doyle noticed that this time the ship stayed alongside the shore for far longer than was usual or prudent. He had seen several Burmese civilians coming aboard and others leaving. Then the captain addressed everyone over the ship's tannoy.

'I have to tell you that our Burmese crew have deserted,' he explained. 'The Japanese are apparently less than a mile away. If we stay we will all be captured, and as we're totally unarmed, I'll leave you to imagine our treatment. But without a crew we cannot sail. I appeal to everyone well enough to report below decks to the engine room – *at once.*'

Immediately Doyle went down the dirty companionway to the engine room. The Chief Engineer, a Scot, ordered them to stoke the fires beneath the boilers. They shovelled like maniacs; men with arms in slings, legs bound to wooden splints, men with head and body wounds, even a man blinded in a grenade attack. Some collapsed with a great flurry of shovels; one man died, others broke down with the pain of wounds opened by their efforts. And for every one who fell out, another, often even more gravely injured, took his place.

Slowly the head of steam built up; needles in the pressure gauges trembled on their springs. The paddles began to turn, sluggishly at first, and then with greater speed and confidence.

But these amateur stokers could not maintain their efforts; the ship's speed gradually fell because of lowered steam pressure. Everyone realized that they were only delaying the moment of capture, but at least this was a positive achievement. While they remained free, there was always the hope that the fortunes of war would favour them; a faint hope, agreed, but better than none, much better than surrender and defeat.

There was a nightmare quality of disbelief about the voyage, with the crackle of gunfire now heard plainly from both banks of the river, and the constant roar and sweep of Japanese Zero fighters overhead on their way north to take out another target.

With so many men, women, children aboard, all seriously ill, some dying of unknown fevers as well as the ever-present malaria, conditions became foul. Swarms of black flies had settled on the vomit and excrement of the sick, and completely covered the suppurating open sores of the wounded.

Doyle and others fit enough to move hosed the decks regularly, but this meant hosing patients who lay there crying out in agony, begging to be left alone. Then came the unmistakeable symptoms of cholera. Two men, obviously suffering from this, were carried to the aft end, where, separated as far as possible from everyone else, they lay on the bare boards of the deck without treatment or hope.

An army engineer in charge of the stokers now reported to the captain that coal was running out. If they did not berth soon the steamer would just drift on the tide, with the captain unable to control her progress forwards or backwards, a useless iron hulk on an enemy river. She would then become a prey to the currents and an easy victim to be towed inshore by any Japanese craft. The captain fully realized this situation, and he had to admit that it was hopeless. He decided to stop his ship while sufficient head of steam remained to control her.

In peacetime this paddle steamer, and others of the Irrawaddy Flotilla Company, would ply between Rangoon and the railhead north of Mandalay, where the river grew shallow. They could see the railhead from the steamer. Now the marines and other servicemen secured the vessel fore and aft to bollards and helped the more seriously injured ashore. Many were too ill to walk and had to be carried on the backs of fitter men, or on crude stretchers made of bamboos lashed together. Some were too ill to be moved at all and simply lay delirious with fever, or in a coma from poisoned wounds.

At first Doyle had the greatest difficulty in walking. Then he bound more bandages around his feet and ankles so that he did not have to walk on bare feet and found that he could hobble less painfully. He and the few remaining members of Force Viper stayed together; all marines, without an officer, a sergeant or a corporal among them. They walked off the path to a small loading area and then a railway platform.

A mass of abandoned trucks and empty tankers were jammed one behind the other in the sidings. The platform was crowded with people sitting on bundles of belongings or just squatting on their heels, staring vacantly ahead. They had marched so far and lost so much that all initiative had disappeared. They could only wait, minds switched off, until someone told them what their next move must be, or events galvanized them into action or reaction.

The marines walked along the platform, through the crowds, because at the far end they saw a train and a steam engine. Faint wisps of steam played at the exhaust, but there was no engine driver and no stoker.

An army padre seemed to be the only officer. He called the marines to him. Indian and British soldiers also gathered around him.

'I've just had a warning, passed from some local Burmese official,' the padre explained.

'If we are not out of this station within ten minutes, the Japanese are going to bomb it. There are hundreds of people already on the train and, as you can see for yourself, as many on the platform – women, children, Indians, Burmese, British, Chinese. If what the man says is true, and I have no reason to doubt his word, there will be a fearful massacre. I have been trying to find anyone who can drive a locomotive, but these refugees are too far gone to help me. Can any of you drive a train?'

He looked hopefully from one man to the next.

One soldier stepped forward.

'I used to work on the London Midland & Scottish, sir,' he explained. 'I was a signalman. I've been in the cab often enough. I know the routine. I reckon I can drive an engine, but we need to get up steam. There is no coal here. I've had a look in the tender.'

'Will it burn wood?' the padre asked him.

The man nodded.

'Should do,' he said.

'Then let's gather some wood,' said Doyle.

The railhead was surrounded by trees, but it was impossible to cut them down, trim them, saw up the trunks into logs. For one thing there was no time; for another, they had no saws.

'Break up the station,' Doyle suggested.

The wooden seats, the railings, anything.'

Fatigue parties set to work, pulling planks off walls, jamming them into a doorway and leaning against them until they broke into manageable lengths, then tossing them into the tender. As Doyle took charge of one of these groups, he suddenly became aware that the pain in his legs and feet was growing. The prospect of action, of survival, had effectively blanketed the agony of the septic untreated wounds. But the act of walking in bandaged feet on hot concrete and the wooden boards of the platform, with splinters occasionally piercing his flesh, made him realize his own predicament. The other marines and soldiers wore boots, or at least rubber-soled canvas shoes. They could march or fetch and carry. He could barely walk.

He sat down on one of the few remaining benches and removed the bandages to examine his ankles. They were cut and bleeding. The bandages were filthy from walking on them, and sodden and stinking with pus. He had to treat his injuries in some way or they would turn gangrenous, and he knew that then he would die. He removed the bandages, washed his feet and ankles under a station tap, rinsed out the bandages as best he could and bound them tightly around his legs, so that they looked like the mummified feet of a high-class

Chinese woman in the nineteenth century. The pain was still great, but at least his ankles felt cooler. For the moment he had reduced the inflammation.

By the time he had finished, the train was ready to move. He climbed up in the cab with the former signalman and two marines who were going to stoke. They stripped off their filthy shirts in the heat of the cab. The metal floor was uncomfortably warm through Doyle's bandages. Through sooty windows he could see the dirty boiler, and smoke, thick and black from the burning wood, rising from the funnel. The signalman opened various cocks, spun wheels, moved levers, and slowly, very slowly, the train began to move forward.

At the first movement, dozens, possibly hundreds more people on the platform leaped into the carriages, pushing their way desperately into the mass of passengers already there. Others stood on the running-boards, hanging on to door handles, or keeping their place by arms through open windows. The train slowly gathered speed, but the best they could manage was about 12 miles an hour. The boiler ate wood at a tremendous rate, and the wood only produced a fraction of the heat from coal. When they approached a gradient, even a slight one, the engine simply had not the power to pull the heavily overcrowded train up the hill. It slowed and finally stopped with a great and impotent roaring of steam. The padre and Doyle and others climbed down on to the track.

'Everyone out!' they shouted, beating the doors with sticks and pieces of wood. 'Everybody out!'

When only a few moved, they physically pulled others off the running-board, and tipped people out from the compartments, to relieve the weight. Thus lightened, the train moved slowly on to the top of the gradient. There it stopped while the passengers ran alongside to catch it up and climb aboard. This was repeated at every hill, and each time the train climbed the gradient more slowly than it had climbed the previous one. The boiler was running out of steam, because the wood had been used up, and no more was available. Finally, it became clear that the train could run for only a few more miles before it was forced to stop altogether. As it stood poised on the top of a hill, the padre climbed up on top of the cab and addressed everyone.

'It seems we have two alternatives,' he said. 'We can either stay in the train and go on until the wood is finished and we have to walk, or we can leave here. This is a decision that everyone must make themselves. It can literally be a matter of life or death.

'I am prepared to lead as many as wish to

follow me overland to the Assam/Bengal border. I reckon that this involves a trek of between 500 or 600 miles, so it is not a walk to embark on lightly. I have a compass, however, and I have served in Burma for several years and know the country, at least for the first 15 or 20 miles. I cannot guarantee that we will reach the border, but at least we will be heading in the right direction. Anyone who wants to come with me, fall out on the left.'

Most of the soldiers joined him; so did a number of civilians. He was an officer and a minister of religion; it seemed that he spoke with authority. The alternative, to stay with the train, seemed singularly unattractive. The marines discussed the matter. Doyle wanted to stay where he was – largely because he knew that, with his ankles, he could not hope to keep up with the marchers wearing shoes. The other marines agreed with him. The padre did not.

'You've no compass. You are totally unarmed – and if you can't march now, you can't march when the train stops. What possible hope have you got of escaping if you stay on the train?'

'The next main station is Myitkyina, the end of the line,' Doyle replied. 'There's an airstrip there, and very likely a shuttle service of planes to India. It makes more sense to fly than hobble six hundred miles.'

'We're nearer to India here than you'll be in Myitkyina,' the padre pointed out. 'Knowing the chaos at all the other airstrips in Burma, I don't imagine that Myitkyina will be any better. It may even be a great deal worse, because so many other people will have the same idea. I don't want to persuade anyone against their will, but I most earnestly suggest that the best chance is to come overland with me.

'Remember that the monsoon will set in within a matter of days. Then everything will change overnight. The roads, such as they are, will become raging rivers. Paddy fields will be lakes. The jungle grows twice as fast and is twice as thick. And leeches get into your boots and batten onto your flesh. I know the country and I know what it's like in the monsoon. I can't promise anything, but I think that to leave now with me offers the best hope of survival.'

Doyle could accept the argument, but he remained doubtful. Any sort of vehicle was preferable to him than walking.

'Aren't they evacuating the wounded from Myitkyina?' he asked.

'So the rumour was in Mandalay. But this whole campaign is full of rumours. We don't know the facts. You can bet your life they'll be very short of planes, and if you're stuck at the camp there, you'll be much worse off than if you leave here. For one thing, you'll have farther to walk, and for another, your route will lie slap across head-hunters' country. With your feet, Doyle, you haven't a very good chance of making it.'

'Maybe there will be a headquarters of some kind in Myitkyina? Anyhow, sir, the longer I can keep the weight off my legs, the better chance I will have.'

'As you wish,' said the padre.

He formed the others – upwards of a hundred men – into three lines. All looked towards him for guidance: he was their main hope of survival, the officer, the man with the compass. The signalman leaned out of the cab to him.

'Goodbye, sir,' he said. 'Good luck!'

'May God go with you all,' replied the padre. 'I hope that we will meet again, and serve again, and give thanks together to God for our deliverance.' Some people murmured 'Amen.'

The train started to move forward as the padre waved farewell. Doyle leaned out of the cab, watching the group who had elected to walk with him. As the train gathered speed, they began to move off. Some had sticks and staves, because they could not walk unaided. Others were helped by comrades. None of them looked back. That was the last Doyle saw of them. His memory was of a little group going steadfastly on into the green mist-capped hills.

With so many people now off the train, the engine had a lot less load to pull, and its performance perked up marginally. Now, those who were still aboard could stay in the train on all but the steepest inclines. Finally, with their stock of wood almost finished, they came into Myitkyina, the nearest Burmese town of consequence to China, and so possessing considerable trading significance.

To its west lay amber and jade mines. Sapphires came from the north and rubies from the south. Myitkyina was the most northerly town in Burma, and the country's northern rail terminus. It stood on a plain, with mountains on three sides, reaching to a height of 15,000 feet. India lay to its west, China to the east and the Japanese to the south. The country round about was virtually uninhabited, save for small villages, often little more than a handful of wooden huts built on the edge of the road.

In May, when the monsoon started, until October when it ended, it would endure almost constant rain. In Britain, the average rainfall over twelve months of the year is slightly over 30 inches. In Myitkyina and the surrounding country, more than 200 inches of rain – sometimes considerably more – fell every year.

An American volunteer group had been established in Myitkyina to help run a hospital that covered an enormous area of tents and bamboo bashas. The camp seemed full of British, American, Chinese and Indian troops, but either they were on duty here or they were stragglers, like the marines, waiting for orders. There was no headquarters of any kind that Doyle could find to issue him and his small party with orders – or even weapons.

Myitkyina possessed a long airstrip, and a number of aircraft were waiting to take off, but Doyle saw that they were so crammed with refugees that some could not leave the ground. The aircraft would race up and down the runway in an exercise of desperation and futility, and some planes that had succeeded in taking wing had not flown very far. In the scrub around the airfield lay the wreckage of several, shot down almost as soon as they were airborne. Clearly there was no hope for the marines, without any priority whatever, or any urgent reason to set them above others who had been waiting for days or weeks to go.

Perhaps he should have followed the padre's advice and gone with the earlier party. Doyle discussed the matter with the other marines. Would they be willing to take the chance of marching over the hills with him? They shook their heads. The prospect held no attractions for them. There was little hope of them being able to march for long periods, because most could barely walk a hundred yards each, let alone cover perhaps 500 miles. They were weak from dysentery and malaria, with odd compounded fevers, ulcerated legs, septic wounds. Their best chance must be to stay in the tented hospital and receive what treatment they could. Then, at some unspecified future date, more planes might arrive, or they would feel fit, enough to march.

'Time's against us,' Doyle told them. 'Every day the Japanese are coming nearer. And then there's the monsoon to consider.'

He was more disturbed than he cared to admit, even to himself, at the sight of the overcrowded aircraft. And he noted that the ones that did manage to take off successfully did not always return. Either they were intercepted and shot down, or the pilots decided to keep them in the relative safety of India rather than risk flying back to Myitkyina. Without aircraft, Doyle reckoned they had only two choices: stay where they were and await capture – or march out and hope to survive the journey.

The sound of gunfire seemed closer every day, and the feeling of tension was rising hour by hour. Everyone who could leave had already done so. Dogs roamed the streets, howling for masters who had abandoned them. Houses had been broken into, but often their contents had proved too heavy or too cumbersome to carry away. The looters' lives were more important to them than loot, which they abandoned in the streets.

There was little treatment available for most people, because what drugs the hospital possessed were needed for men with terrible wounds and amputations. But Doyle had his wounds dressed daily and covered with clean lint and bandages, and the inflammation had decreased. A Roman Catholic priest made the rounds of the tents every day, speaking to patients well enough to hear him or conduct a conversation.

He was an old man who had been a missionary in Burma for many years. The hem of his white cassock was stained with flecks of blood from the wounded. A crucifix on a black ribbon around his neck had been worn smooth by the fingers of those who touched or held it, believers and unbelievers alike: it was a totem, a talisman, a symbol and a source of comfort to men almost without hope.

Doyle was a Catholic and the priest took an interest in him because he and his comrades were the only Royal Marines the priest had ever met.

Each morning Doyle hobbled around the perimeter outside the tents trying to glean any information, and to prove to himself that his condition was improving. Every day brought new dangers in delay, but he was still clearly unfit to attempt such an enormous trek. One day he saw the priest talking to two soldiers. He beckoned to Doyle to join them.

'These soldiers have been asking me about their chances of walking back to India through the jungle,' the priest explained.

'And what are they?' Doyle asked him.

'Negligible,' the priest replied shortly. 'In my opinion they haven't a chance. I've been out here for more than forty years and seen forty monsoons. The forty-first is due to start any day Have any of you seen a monsoon?'

They all shook their heads.

'Then I'll tell you what to expect. This whole dry plateau here will become a lake of mud. The water will sweep through each tent. When you get out of bed, you will walk through it up to your ankles. Pots, pans, mats, just float about. You may hang up your boots at night, and next morning they will be green with mildew. Every track you walk on now, that fills your lungs with dust at each step, will become a roaring river. Rivers like the Irrawaddy and the Chindwin, quite navigable in normal times – people even swim across them – will become raging torrents that no one can cross.

'Everything on them, or even near them – families, animals, huts – will be swept away. It just rains and rains and rains. Leeches – you don't even notice them in the dry weather – appear like small slugs and worm their way into your boots. They're tiny little things, like maggots at first, but they gorge on your blood and swell up to the size of a cigar. They possess such a powerful sucker to stick to your flesh that you have to burn them off with the end of a lighted cigarette. If you only cut them off with a knife, the wound will start to weep, and it won't stop.'

'But lots of people *have* made it, Father,' said Doyle.

'Some, agreed. Many have started on the journey, but only a fraction finish it. And they were marching out in the dry season, when the going was easier.'

'Which route did they take?' asked one of the soldiers.

'Due north.'

'But why north, when India is surely to the west?'

'Because the jungle is much thicker to the west. If you go north, you have to beat two enemies, the Japanese and the monsoon. You still have the jungle, but it is slightly less hostile and thick.'

'Would you come with us if we went north, father?'

'No, my son,' the missionary replied. 'My place is here, with the sick and wounded. I have worked here all my adult life. I've known Burmese and Indians who are now in middle age from their childhood. I know

123

their children, as I knew their fathers and mothers. This is my place, here among them. They've seen enough Europeans, who were supposed to protect them, running away to save their own lives. What can they believe in if I do the same? They trust me. I am honoured by their trust. I cannot break it.'

'I understand, Father,' said Doyle. 'But if we go, would you suggest we set out due north from here?'

'I would suggest nothing, Doyle. I have told you my views as to your chances. Your colleagues here asked my opinion, and I have done my best to answer truthfully. *If* I were going, I would go in exactly the opposite direction – south. That's where the Japanese are, of course, but I would still go south until I reached the valley. This has a road of sorts, even motorable in the dry weather. It is not surfaced, of course, for most of the way. In the monsoon nothing goes on it, not even a bullock cart. But it is a track, a known way.'

'How far is the valley from here, sir?'

'Probably 20 miles. Have you got a map?'

'No, sir.'

'A compass?'

'No. Nothing but the clothes I stand up in. What you see me wearing.'

'Then you are going to your death, my son.'

'But you say there is a track, at least. I can

follow that, surely? Like a train line, it'll keep me on the straight and narrow.'

'You seem to think it is like a farm track or a country lane in England. It isn't. The jungle encroaches on it – and may totally obscure whole lengths of it during the monsoon. And other tracks branch off from it to villages, and so on. Without a compass or a guide, you won't know which one to take. They aren't signposted, you know.'

'I know that, sir, but if I stay here I'm likely to be captured. And we all know what happened to the patients in hospital at Hong Kong when the Japs came in.'

'They were bayoneted. Nurses who tried to shield the sick and wounded with their own bodies, to protect them, were bayoneted as well,' the priest replied. 'We can expect no mercy from the sons of Nippon, but perhaps the Lord has a way.'

'He might have a way to help us,' said Doyle. 'Could you give us your blessing, Father?'

'Willingly, but the decision must be yours. The two courses are about evenly balanced. Let me tell you a story from Somerset Maugham to show you what I mean.

'You naturally enough hope to escape what you think is death here. But you may, of course, not be running away from your destiny, but towards it. There was a rich merchant in Baghdad once, whose servant

125

went into the bazaar, and there he was horrified to see Death, who touched his arm and frightened him. He ran back to his master and said, "Master, I was in the bazaar and Death frightened me. Lend me your fastest horse, I beg you, that I may ride tonight to Samarra and so escape from him."

'"Of course," the master said at once, "It is yours."

'So the servant rode off in great haste, and his master went down to the bazaar and, sure enough, there was Death standing by a stall. And he said to Death: "Why did you frighten my servant this morning?"

'And Death replied: "I did not frighten him, I was just surprised to see him in Baghdad this morning when tonight I have an appointment with him in Samarra."'

'I see,' said Doyle. 'There's not much comfort in that.'

'There's not meant to be,' the priest replied. 'You cannot avoid your destiny. None of us can. But let me also give you a thought from Shakespeare. "Cowards die many times before their death. The valiant never taste of death but once."

'You can stay here wondering whether you are going to die from septic wounds or from fever, from a bomb or a bayonet, or whether you will be captured and maybe die a prisoner. But if you are *meant* to escape, if it is the Lord's will that you should live, you *will* live. Despite all obstacles, all dangers, despite everything set in the way against you.'

'So what is your advice, sir?' asked one of the soldiers. 'Stay or go?'

'You are young and I am old. I can speak from experience, and I have seen hundreds of refugees – thousands – go north, but no one knows how they fared. We have no means of communication with India here. We hope they reached safety, but the odds are overwhelmingly against them. There are not only the hazards of the journey, but also wild animals, and wild men who have often no reason to like Europeans, let alone help them.

'Our role out here was not only to administer a country but to protect it. In the first we succeeded admirably. In the last we have failed lamentably. If you doubt my words, just look about you. But still, you, unarmed and in retreat, can have an important part to play. For you are trained not only in the arts of war, but in the frequently more difficult art of survival.

'These refugees are fleeing without a plan, without preparation, leaving in many cases their whole life's work and possessions behind them. They have not had your training. If you go, you will have the opportunity to help them in ways in which they cannot help themselves. But before you plan such a hazardous journey, you must ask yourself this question. Can you make it? Are you *strong* enough, even if you overcome everything else? That is a matter for each man to decide. I can only wish you well in whatever course you do decide to take. May God be with you if you stay, and go with you if you go.'

He made the sign of the cross.

'Amen,' said Doyle.

The priest walked on into the tent. Doyle turned to his two companions. He did not particularly care for either of them. They were below medium height, thin, with sharp faces. He could not imagine them in the Marines, or even surviving a long and arduous march. But surely any company was better than none on such an undertaking?

They introduced themselves to each other.

'My name's Jack,' said the first soldier.

'I'm Dick,' said the second.

Doyle noticed they had not given him their surnames. There was, of course, no reason why they should, but somehow their reticence made him slightly uneasy. Was this something they felt necessary to hold back? Were they deserters? Well, that was their affair, not his. The most important matter was whether they stayed in Myitkyina or took a chance by marching out.

'Shall we go?' he asked.

'I reckon,' said Dick.

'When?'

'May as well start tomorrow. Get down towards the valley. Can we find it?'

'Should be dead easy. Just follow the railway line.' said Jack.

'Can we get any food, any gear to take with us?'

He shrugged.

'I've got a revolver,' he replied. 'It's the best argument – if you want to get food from someone.'

'If they have any to give,' said Doyle, remembering the burning buildings on the way north. There might be a chicken here or there, the remains of a sack of rice, but not much more. The Burmese had already proved themselves to be experts at removing anything of value.

'How will you make out without any boots?' Jack asked Doyle. 'It's every man for himself in this, you know.'

'Of course,' agreed Doyle. 'But the whole point is that the three of us have three times as much chance of getting out as one.'

'You reckon?' asked Dick.

'I do reckon,' said Doyle.

'But you start off lame already. Imagine going for a route march back in England without any boots, and your bare feet tied up with bits of bandages and God knows what all. You wouldn't have a hope.'

'It's the only hope,' replied Doyle grimly. 'And I'm going to take it.'

'All right then. That's your affair. We'll see you here, say seven-thirty tomorrow morning. Get a bit of breakfast inside us first, such as it is. You got a watch?'

'No,' said Doyle. 'Have you?'

'No. We could use a watch as a compass. Turn the little hand to the sun, bisect the difference between the minute and the hour hand and you find where north is.'

'I know that,' said Doyle. 'But it's useless knowledge since we haven't got a watch between us.'

'I'll see if I can steal one,' said Dick.

'I wouldn't,' Doyle advised. 'It's no good starting off like that. Some other poor devil may want it for the same purpose as we do.'

'That's his bad luck.'

'I reckon we take our chance,' replied Doyle. 'If we find a dead man with a watch on his wrist, that's a different matter.'

'You're lucky to find a dead man with even his clothes on. The Japanese are bad enough. And what they leave, the Burmese take. You've seen how they treat the dead?'

'No,' said Doyle uneasily, suddenly remembering the three Indians he had seen shot by the firing squad. How long ago had that been? Weeks, months, a lifetime? But the memories of those others who had also seen the shooting would be fresh and long. They could expect no mercy if they fell into their hands.

'I'll tell you what they do. For some reason, Burmese think the teeth are valuable – maybe they make necklaces from them. I don't know. But they go round with a pair of pliers, taking out the teeth of any bodies they find.'

'So long as they're dead,' said Doyle hopefully.

He did not believe this; it had the element of fantasy, make-believe. Or was his reaction one of self-delusion because the story seemed too horrible to believe?

'I've seen them do it when they're not quite dead,' Dick continued. 'They drop a bloody great rock on the bloke's head. Then they take his teeth. Well, be seeing you tomorrow!'

The two soldiers walked away.

Doyle stood looking after them. They were not companions he would have chosen, but then perhaps they might not have chosen him. Yet surely any companions must be better than being on one's own in this unmapped and terrible jungle?

He went into the cookhouse to see whether there was any food he could scrounge for his journey, but he had nothing to carry rice in, and there was no bread, no tins of milk, not even a knife or fork.

He went back to his bed, unwound the bandages from his ankles and regarded his wounds critically. While they were less painful, they did not really show much improvement. The gashes were several inches long on both legs just above the ankles, to the front and the side. Flesh had drawn back so that they looked like mouths. He could see muscle beneath, and the edges of flesh were yellow with pus. They smelled.

He hobbled outside to a tap, rinsed the bandages, stretched them out over the top of a shrub to dry in the sun. Several pairs of boots lay about the tent, taken from dead men's feet, but none would fit him. His feet had swollen and were too tender to push into any of them, and the tongues and tops of all the boots he tried on rubbed against his wounds. It was bad enough to walk fifty yards in his bandages – so how would he manage 500 miles?

Doyle had never been a particularly religious person. As a boy he had not been the most ardent churchgoer or member of the Sunday school, but the priest he had just seen had impressed him deeply. Here was a man who could have presumably escaped weeks earlier, but quite calmly had decided to stay; that was his duty, his calling. He knew he faced possible torture if he was captured. The priest's remark about fleeing from one's destiny only to meet it, and the other quotation about courage, had also impressed Doyle. These were words to live up to, words to remember and live by.

It was a long time since he had prayed. What was he going to ask God, assuming God heard him, assuming even there was a God to hear? He wanted help, guidance; he wanted to live, to reach India, to find headquarters – and then come back to the battle. He knelt down.

'Please help me and my two companions, Jack and Dick, as we set out,' he prayed. 'Give us wisdom to make the right decisions, to follow the right road. And having made that choice, under Your guidance, please give us strength to carry it out.

'I ask this in the name of Jesus Christ, in Whose name I was taught that everything asked can be granted – if it is your wish. I beg of You, please make it Your wish that we all survive.'

He stood up. Outside, the day seemed almost feverishly bright; the monsoon was not far away. Clouds of dust billowed about in the hot acrid wind. The sides of the tent were open and its roof fluttered like a giant khaki sail.

'You're a Plymouth marine,' he heard the Major say. 'You know your headquarters – Plymouth! Get yourself kitted out and back in the fight. No one wins a war by running away.'

Doyle wondered where the Major was. Had he been killed or captured? He had no means of knowing, but his words he would never forget. He would go, and if he did not reach headquarters, at least he would have tried his utmost to do so.

Having made his decision, despite the odds against him with his feet and ankles, Doyle felt curiously content. He was going to go forward; there was no way back.

At half past seven the following morning, after a breakfast of tea with a slice of bread and a small plate of porridge, he waited by the side of the tent for Jack and Dick. They arrived about ten minutes later.

They were now both wearing different boots, not the shabby ones they had worn the previous day: these had good soles and strong laces. They also had bush hats and clean shirts.

'Where d'you get the kit from?' he asked them.

'Won it,' replied Dick laconically 'Blokes in bed didn't seem to have much use for it. We do.'

'I've also won a watch,' said Jack, displaying a gunmetal watch with an expanding chromium-plated strap. The sergeant had it by his bed. People shouldn't leave valuables lying about. Asking for trouble, that is.'

They set off to the station, marching in step and three abreast. Doyle had seen the priest the previous evening as he made his rounds, and explained that they were going to attempt the long march. The priest had told him that the valley was a day's march on a good road for a fit man carrying a full pack. How long would it take him, he wondered.

At the station hundreds of people were sitting morosely on suitcases tied with rope or on bundles of luggage, hoping for the miracle of a train. The only train visible was the one that had brought Doyle into Myitkyina, and this still stood in the sidings, forlorn, derelict and useless. Without coal or a crew, it was simply a mass of metal and wood, a wheeled monument to futility. And even if fuel and a driver could be found, there was nowhere for any train to go; Myitkyina was literally the end of the line.

The three men started to walk south along the railway track. At first they walked on the sleepers, much as children playing a game in a city side street will take long strides from one paving stone to another, taking care to land always on the joints. But Doyle found it difficult to keep up. His companions had boots; he had only bandages around his feet. Each step became an agony. Soon he fell behind. They were walking side by side a few feet ahead of him. Then the gap grew steadily; they were ten feet ahead, then twenty.

At ten minutes to the hour by Dick's watch they all stopped and lay down, concealed in bushes at the side of the track. On the hour they set off again. Miles passed slowly. Zeros soared overhead and they dropped under cover of the jungle in case they were seen and fired on. The fact that they were going south, when all the other refugees appeared to be heading north, could in itself be suspicious.

It was doubtful whether the Japanese pilots ever saw the three figures, and even if they did, they had more important targets in mind. Doyle could hear the crump of bombs falling and a rattle of machine-guns. As they walked, it became more difficult to establish the direction of these sounds. What was ominous, and without argument, was they seemed to be growing louder. This was to be expected, because they were marching towards the Japs, feeling that perhaps they were the only British troops in uniform in that area to be doing so.

For the first few miles Dick and Jack talked to each other in low tones, but soon the heat made them thirsty. Speech became an effort; it was less tiring to walk in silence. By evening, without any water or food, they reached the outskirts of a shattered town.

Here the track divided. The main line went south to Rangoon and the other line petered out into a siding. In peacetime this had been a busy junction. Now the few trucks there were empty, pitted with shell-holes, with their sides down. Whatever goods they had once contained had long ago been looted. Dick wanted to search the town to see whether there was anything worth taking away. They might even find a car or motorcycle. Doyle was against this.

'If the Japs aren't in here yet, then they're all around,' he said. 'We would be walking right into a trap. And you can be sure that if there are any vehicles left, it's only because they haven't any petrol. Let's get farther north for a mile or two and kip down off the road, somewhere quiet.'

The other two looked at each other and shrugged.

'If you say so,' said Dick, as if the matter was of no importance.

A road led north out of the town, metalled at first and then deteriorating to an unmade track. This was the only way north, so they set off along it, past houses with shutters blown off and glass windows shattered; empty frames stared sightlessly at each other across the track. Here and there a car or truck had been abandoned, with doors swinging in the wind, boots and bonnets open. Whatever could be looted had been taken: batteries, lights, wheels and tyres.

They trudged on in silence, and gradually the houses became less numerous and of poorer quality, soon little more than wooden huts built up on stilts. Here and there a hog snorted and grunted at their approach, and fled away under the house or into the jungle. The heat began to die from the day, and soon the mosquitoes would be out, humming and whining around them. Then there would be the sudden, brief tropical dusk and darkness, when it would be impossible to move.

They found a place to halt about two miles north. Here the track they were following joined another narrower track that led into the heart of the jungle. Between the two was an area of trodden elephant grass. They moved through this and, protected by a screen of thick bushes, lay down. Dick and Jack took off their boots, wriggled their toes, grateful for the cool air on tired hot feet, wrinkled and soft with sweat, sandpapered by the dust of the march.

Doyle unwound the bandages and flexed his tortured ankles. Walking for such a distance had worn right through the bottom of the bandages, so when he replaced them he wound as many layers around his feet as he could. In another few miles, at this rate of wear, he would be marching barefoot. But what happened on the morrow was a problem for that day. For the moment it was enough that they were still alive. This must be a bonus. The morning and the evening had been the first day. He said a silent prayer of thankfulness. They were also about 20 miles nearer the advancing Japanese than when they started out, but now they were set on the route north. And at the end of that road, he would find headquarters, proper treatment for his wounds, and the prospect of returning fit, fighting fit.

They had found a place to rest, but lacking a stream or a well nearby. Doyle's mouth was dry, his tongue like hot leather, and he had a headache from marching in the sun without a hat, and with the sun in his eyes.

He lay down wearily. The other two men lay down to his left. No one spoke. Doyle had meant to ask how they thought they should find any food and water in the morning, but he was so exhausted, he fell asleep with the question still on his mind.

While he slept, he dreamed. He was back in his safe, warm little room in Middlesbrough. He could hear the siren at Dorman Long's and the clatter of trains outside his bedroom window. And then the dream faded and he was suddenly awake. He looked around him.

Where were Jack and Dick?

Perhaps they had gone to relieve themselves – or to forage for food, to find the nearest stream? He heard the ominous rumble of distant guns and then, much nearer, the distinctive high-pitched chattering that he knew from harsh experience was the sound of Japanese machine guns. It seemed too risky to call out, so he asked in as loud a voice as he dared, 'Jack. Dick. You about? You OK?'

There was no answer. A bird, disturbed by his voice, began to chirp above his head, calling out with a shrill 'caw, caw, caw'. Doyle stood up. He was stiff and his joints ached, and red ants and mosquitoes had bitten his feet and his bare legs, the back of his neck and the backs of his hands. The flesh was puffy and swollen, his mouth still felt dry, and his head still hurt. He hoped that the mosquitoes had not been malarial, or he would feel infinitely worse within a matter of hours.

Where the devil could his companions be? He searched around the clearing, then up and down the road, even along the jungle track for fifty yards. But there was neither sight nor sound of them. It took him some time to accept what deep down in his heart he had guessed the moment he had woken. They had deserted him. He was not their type, with them but not of them. They were fit and he was lame. They had gone ahead on their own. It had seemed far safer to attempt the march north with two companions; three chances instead of one, to cut the risk by the same ratio. Now he was on his own again: one man, one chance.

He stood for a moment, wondering exactly what he should do. He knew that the road, such as it was, led vaguely to the north, but if it divided farther up, left and right, which fork should he take? Without a compass or a watch he could only guess, but with the sun now moving swiftly up the sky, he guessed roughly where north lay. It was a very approximate estimate, and even if north lay through the jungle, how would he know when to branch west to reach India?

He shook his head from side to side, banged his ears with the palms of his hands to try and clear his brain. The horror of the situation was almost too much to assimilate. Surely he could not really be alone, on his own in the Burma jungle?

When he had been with other marines in Rangoon, or aboard *Rita*, or up in Myitkyina, he had been one of a group, part of a human mosaic. He had people to joke with, to rally when events were going against them. They could do the same for him. But now he had no one to rely on, no one to talk to or joke with; no one whose opinion he could seek, whose memory he could jog to recall a past experience shared.

Then he had been armed; there were tommy-guns, rifles, grenades; aboard the launch a Vickers machine-gun, even a radio. Now he had nothing to defend himself with, let alone to attack any aggressor. He did not even possess the basic eating tools of every fighting man: a knife, a fork, a spoon. He had his shirt, rotting and torn and filthy; underpants, khaki shorts. He had neither

141

socks nor boots. His feet were bound up in bandages that had already deteriorated into dirty, stinking strips of rag. He did not possess a hat to protect his head from the heat of the sun, which by all teaching could drive a bareheaded man to madness. (The theory widely held was that the sun could literally boil a person's brains.)

Doyle tried to force himself to think coherently, to work out a plan. He could go south again to the junction, follow the railway line back to Myitkyina and admit defeat.

And if he took this easier course, what would happen then? Explain that his companions had abandoned him and he was afraid, unable, unwilling to try to march out on his own? However he tried to explain away this decision, it was a defeat to him personally, and obliquely to the Corps of Royal Marines. Almost certainly he would be captured, and either kept as a prisoner of war, or what seemed more likely to him in his desperate state, he would be killed, possibly bayoneted, a living target for Japanese recruits.

That was one option.

Another was to keep on the course the priest had suggested, and go north, alone. Surely he would not be the only refugee on this track? There must be other groups, civilians or perhaps soldiers, who he could join? If this was the main route out of

Burma, he could not conceivably be the only person using it. That made sense, and comforted him.

Wild beasts might attack him, but he had read somewhere that wild beasts were in greater fear of man than man need be of them. An encouraging thought; he hoped he would never have to put it to the test.

A third option seemed barely worth considering. This was to stay where he was and hope that another group marching north found him, and then he could latch on to them and become one of a group again, seeking safety in numbers. But such a possibility was by no means certain. The refugees had a start on him. He was more likely to catch up with them than to be overtaken. This choice also carried the risk that increased with every hour he delayed: a Japanese advance party might find him, and on his own he would have no chance at all. The only possible decision was to go north – and as quickly as possible.

If he kept straight on, assuming he survived, where would he come out? In China? Tibet? He wished he had spent more time in geography lessons at school. But it was too late for that now. It was too late really for anything but to start putting as much distance as possible between the Japanese and himself.

He searched around the clearing for

anything he could use as a weapon. There was not even a stick. Finally he broke a branch off a tree, peeled off its auxiliary shoots and used this as a stave. It would help him to walk, and if he were attacked it would be better than his bare fists. At least that was a comforting thought, but against any armed man the willowy branch would be useless. However, that was a negative thought; he must not let such defeatism occupy his mind. What did the song advise? Accentuate the positive. That must be his motto.

He came out of the clearing and started to walk north along the dusty road. He scratched himself where dust had penetrated the threadbare material of his shirt; it felt as though he was sandpapering his flesh. His fingers went right through parts of the cloth. He rubbed worms of dust and sweat out of his soaking skin. He must find a cleaner shirt somewhere – but where? How different things were back in Middlesbrough, when he could walk into Binns department store and buy a shirt, any shirt! His mind followed this train of thought. He rather fancied a striped shirt and a Brocklehurst tie, one of those with a small silk tassel on them. So far as he remembered, no other tie had a similar decoration. They were very smart, but pricey, half-a-crown and three-and-sixpence – a lot when a shirt might only cost twice as much.

He seemed to be dreaming as he walked. This could be the result of hunger and thirst and the blaze of the sun in his eyes. He came to a wooden house, built like the rest on stilts and standing a few feet off the track. He went underneath the floor, amid piles of dung from animals, and straw where they had been lying; flies buzzed. He climbed the steps to the verandah. Nothing there. He went into the first room. That had been stripped of everything anyone could carry away. Looters had left a bed and the frame of a chair; nothing else. There were hooks in the wall for hurricane lamps, but of course no hurricane lamps. He went into the back premises. The house did not have running water.

He went down the stairs again, round to the rear of the building. Shielded by a screen was a well with a wooden cover. A metal scoop hung from a chain; the table on which it had once stood had disappeared. He tried to rip the chain from its fastening, but he could not do so, and he had nothing he could use to lever it away. He lowered the scoop into the well and drew out some water. He smelled it cautiously; it seemed fresh enough. He had heard stories of Japanese poisoning wells with the bodies of dogs, or even of human beings.

He tasted it with the tip of his tongue, then he put the scoop to his lips and drank greedily. Immediately sweat started out of his parched skin. He still felt as though he had drunk nothing. He dipped the scoop in the well for a second time, and this time drank more slowly. Then he poured water over his hands and flung a scoopful in his face, wiping it dry with the rags of his shirt. He removed the bandages from his feet, poured cold water over the wounds, and replaced the bandages. Again he tugged at the metal scoop, but he could not remove it from the chain. He would have to leave it, although he knew how valuable it would be on his journey.

He searched around the back of the hut in an outhouse. Some sacks were piled here. They could have been used for carrying rice or sugar, for they were of a thin weave. He took off his shirt – it literally came away in strips in his hands as he pulled it over his head – and threw the pieces to one side. Then he selected the longest, cleanest sack and shook the dust out of it. How to make holes for his head and his arms when he had no knife? He saw a nail sticking out of the wall, and he pushed this through the edge of the sack and then pulled it roughly towards him. The sack tore in a jagged line. He did the same thing on the other side, then the centre, and then put the sack over his head and pushed his arms through the holes.

He felt like some grotesque in a music-hall act, a stage country bumpkin wearing a fertiliser sack instead of a shirt. But who was there to laugh at him now? He wished he had a companion – anyone – to do so. He smiled at his own predicament. If the lads back at Stonehouse barracks could see him now! If he could see *them* now. He wondered where they all were. How many had survived? In Ceylon, the Maldives? Perhaps others, like him, were also on their own in Burma.

He left the house and began to walk up the road feeling more cheerful. The water had revived him and refreshed him. He was making an early start, too, which was a good thing. He remembered the Master-at-Arms at Plymouth expounding on the virtues of early rising. He had served in Gibraltar and he would shout: 'It's bloody late! Eight o'clock at least, and not a whore in the house washed! Not a jerry emptied – and the street full of Spanish captains! *Get a move on!*'

He'd get a move on all right if he were here, thought Doyle, and instinctively stepped out at a smarter pace. He was accustomed to the pain in his ankles now, and the fact that the bandages had all but worn through. The soft dust on which he walked had the consistency of warm yellowish flour: it formed a cushion for his feet and billowed up around his ankles.

A couple of miles along the road, outside another village without a name, Doyle saw three cars, half off the road, half in the jungle. Two had been looted and were missing their wheels and instruments. Their bonnets and boots were open, the batteries had gone, together with those parts of the engine the locals could carry away. The other car had so far not been touched. Doyle guessed that the Burmese had taken all they could carry, and would return to deal with this.

The ignition key was still in the lock. He turned it, and the fuel gauge, as he had thought, registered zero. The refugees must have driven these cars until their petrol was exhausted and then gone ahead on foot with what they could carry. He unlocked the boot; it was empty. The inside of the car was thick with typed papers torn out of loose-leaf books. Doyle scrabbled through them, thinking that underneath there might be a fork or a knife, something he could use. The dashboard cubby holes were empty, so were the door pockets, but under the driver's seat his fingers touched a cold, hard serrated edge. He pulled out a Smith & Wesson .38 revolver, and held it in his hand for a moment, drawing comfort from the blue purposeful metal. Then he broke it. There were only two shells in the cylinder. He snapped the revolver shut again, pushed it under the belt of his shorts, beneath his shirt. Two rounds. One for an enemy and, in the last extremity, if he were wounded or if he broke a leg, or some other similar catastrophe befell him which could mean a slow, lingering and painful death, one for himself. He set off again on his way north.

Up ahead of him he saw a crowd of dark-skinned men wearing cotton trousers and dhotis, and women in brightly-coloured saris. Some of the men were pushing handcarts, and one a pram laden with bundles of belongings. They were moving at a very slow pace. Doyle overtook them, despite his bandaged feet. They looked at him with lacklustre eyes. Their faces were drawn and weary. The women wore tiny gold ornaments in their nostrils and had red caste marks on their foreheads. He waved a greeting.

'Good morning,' he said, as though he were back in Middlesbrough.

A middle-aged Indian pushing a handcart replied courteously.

'Good morning to you,' he said. 'Where are you from?'

'Rangoon,' said Doyle. 'And you?'

'Pegu. We're off the main road here. It seemed safer.'

'How long have you been marching?' Doyle asked him.

'A week. We had bad luck. The Japanese bombed us. Several were killed. Others have fallen out. They could not keep up.'

'Where are you heading for?'

The man shrugged. He had no plan,

simply the desire to escape, to survive. He wore a watch and so Doyle discovered that it was earlier than he thought, seven o'clock in the morning. Every so often he asked the time. When the man said it was ten to eight, Doyle announced that he was stopping.

'What for?' asked the Indian in surprise.

'March discipline,' Doyle explained. 'If you keep marching endlessly, you wear yourself out. But if you march for 50 minutes and then take ten minutes rest at the roadside, your feet a bit higher up than your head if you can, to let the blood flow back, you will last twice as long – and only feel half as tired. Like this.'

Doyle moved to the roadside and lay down on his back, feet on a small boulder, his hands under his head. The Indian said something in Hindustani to the others. They stopped in a straggling bunch and stared at Doyle. Then they followed his example. Ten minutes later, they started off again at a much sharper pace.

At ten minutes to noon they all stopped in the shade of some trees. The Indian, who seemed to be in charge, gave orders to others. They lit a fire. Someone produced an aluminium pan from a pushcart. Two younger members of the party carried it through the jungle and came back with it full of water. They had found a stream. Doyle smelled the water. It seemed fresh, for running water was always safer than water taken from a pond or a well. Even so, they boiled it, and brewed up some tea. The Indian offered Doyle a mug and then some chapattis and dhal, a mixture of chopped vegetables in a yellowish sauce.

Doyle was not attracted by the colour, but the taste made up for its appearance, and only when he ate did he realize how desperately hungry he had been.

The man explained that in Pegu he had been a shopkeeper. He hoped to return to that trade, but when? Who could say? In the meantime all his savings were still in the bank, because the bank in Pegu, like the banks in Rangoon, had shut its doors precipitately as the Japanese approached. However, he had a letter from the manager in his pocket, confirming the amount to his credit, and he had confidence that when he reached India, as he was equally sure he would, then the nearest branch of that bank there would honour his debt.

'And your plans?' he asked Doyle.

'To return to headquarters, get kitted out, and fight again.'

'Where's headquarters?'

'Plymouth,' retorted Doyle.

'Plymouth?' repeated the Indian. 'I had a brother in the merchant navy who went to Plymouth once. Fine town.'

'A city.' said Doyle.

'Of course, a city. But a long way from here.'

'Well, we're going in the right direction,' said Doyle. 'At least, I hope we are.'

He stood up to signify that the rest break was over. The others struggled to their feet, washed the aluminium pan, stamped out the fire and set off again. The pace was slow, because several of the older members of the group tired quickly and fell back. Doyle guessed they were barely covering three miles an hour. At this rate, the Japanese could overtake them within days at the most. He explained his worries to the Indian, who agreed.

'But what can we do?' he asked. 'We are limited by the speed of the older ones to keep up and the little children. It is different for a single man. You know what your Rudyard Kipling wrote?'

'No,' said Doyle. Kipling had not figured greatly in his pre-war reading.

'I will tell you. He knew the East, my friend. He said: "Down to Gehenna, or up to the Throne, he travels fastest who travels alone."'

'Where exactly is Gehenna?' asked Doyle, not quite comprehending the drift of the man's thinking.

'A valley south-west of Jerusalem that used to be the scene of human sacrifices. The Gospels call it a place where both soul and body are destroyed.'

'You are a Christian?'

'Yes,' said the man. 'I am, and what I am trying to tell you in a roundabout way – which is how many of us in the East prefer to give advice, rather than come directly to the point, as you in the West sometimes choose – is that if you are on your own, you will travel far faster than if you stay with us.

'We are all going through Gehenna now, my friend. You are young and single, while we are made up of young, old, middle-aged, and, like ships in a convoy, we have to keep to the pace of the slowest. There is no need for all of us to perish. You go on. Take some food with you.'

'I have nothing to give you in return. I've no money to pay for it. Nothing.'

'You have given us something better than money. You have taught us that we need to rest every hour. That is something we did not know before, something that gives us a better chance. There is not much we have to give you in return, but what we have, you are welcome to.'

He dug down into the recesses of the pushcart and brought up a small parcel wrapped in a white linen cloth.

'A pack of chapattis,' he said. 'In this cloth they will keep soft. They contain a lot of goodness, my friend. More energy, I believe, than in one of the steaks you English seem

153

to like.'

'Thank you,' said Doyle, much touched by the Indian's generosity. 'Do you have a compass to set your course?'

'No, my friend. The stars at night and the sun in the day. These are our guides. If we think the road veers too much to the left or the right, we follow the opposite course.'

'Let me see your watch again,' said Doyle. The man bared his wrist and Doyle explained how he could find north by aiming the watch at the sun. The Indian was intrigued.

'So that is something else you have taught us. All my adult life I have been a believer in peace, a follower of the Mahatma. But maybe the military are wiser than I imagined if they teach such useful things. When we stop next time, I will bid you good-day. And may God go with you.'

'A priest said that only the other day,' said Doyle.

'God is your best guide,' the Indian assured him gravely. 'In these unhappy circumstances, the only one.'

'Are all these people with you Christians?'

'Oh, no. Some are Hindus, Moslems. But our little party is a kind of microcosm of all religions, if you like. All of us are on life's journey, hoping for the same goal. In this case, safety.'

At the next stop Doyle left them and

pressed ahead as fast as he could on his lame feet. He felt cheered by this odd meeting. As a boy he had read Bunyan's *Pilgrim's Progress* and he remembered how Christian had undertaken a hazardous journey and on the way encountered various people who either helped or hindered him, but in the end he had reached his goal. Doyle had every intention of doing the same. These thoughts replaced worries about the condition of his feet. Since he had no means to count the hours now, he stopped when he felt weary, and at each stop he took off the bandages.

Eventually he had to admit that it would be impossible to go on any further with them around his feet. They had disintegrated into thin shreds of gauze that came to pieces in his hands as he attempted to retie them. He threw them away, massaged his feet, and examined the wounds. They were no better, possibly no worse, or, more realistically, not very much worse.

He opened the linen square the Indian had given him, took out two chapattis and ate them. Then he put the remainder of the chapattis in the back pocket of his shorts, and carefully tore the linen square into thin strips and bound these like bandages around his feet.

Refreshed in mind and body, and feeling curiously elated without any reason whatever for this new and welcome optimism, he set off again. By dusk he was several miles up the road and it was time to find somewhere to sleep. It had been one thing sleeping with the two other soldiers just off the road, because there were three of them and, even if attacked in their sleep, they could put up some kind of a fight. But on his own, as the sun fell down the sky, Doyle began to feel increasingly anxious.

The optimism brought on by unexpected companionship and food began to desert him. He felt lonely, vulnerable and afraid. He desperately wanted to find some house or shack or bamboo basha where he would feel safe, but of course such a feeling would be illusory. No one was safe in the jungle, even in a crowd. Apart from the enemy on two feet, there were wild animals, poisonous fruits and thorns: he was a hostage to a thousand foes. He might not be any safer, but, surrounded by walls, even if only of bamboo, he would have the feeling of being protected, and not this fearful sensation of being totally alone, unarmed. But he could not see any houses, not even a bamboo shack.

The track grew steadily narrower, and the jungle on either side pressed in like two living green walls. He could only go forwards or backwards, and he found himself walking more slowly, taking shorter steps, as though he feared going too fast. Could this mean he was afraid of what the priest would call his destiny?

He was pondering the problem when the road turned sharply to the right. Twenty yards away a man was leaning against a tree, arms folded. He was Burmese and wore a check *longyi,* a short-sleeved shirt, and a kind of bandana around his head.

He stood looking along the track towards Doyle, almost as though he was expecting him, waiting for him, as though any moment he would come forward with hand outstretched and say, 'William Doyle, I presume?'

Doyle came level with him, nodded a greeting. The man asked one word in English.

'English?'

Doyle nodded. The man grinned and jerked his head to the left. Doyle could see that a small pathway opened between the thick foliage. The friendliness of the stranger touched Doyle. It was refreshing to have human contact again. Doyle followed him along the path. It led to a clearing in a village; the usual houses on stilts with goats and chickens underneath them. A dog watched him with yellow baleful eyes.

The man indicated one of the larger houses, and went up the creaking wooden stairway. Doyle followed him. Inside, four other Burmese were sitting cross-legged on the floor, smoking cheroots. The man who had met Doyle introduced the oldest of the four.

'Our headman,' he said.

Doyle bowed; he didn't know what to say. The headman removed a cheroot, glanced at Doyle quizzically through a thin blue haze of bitter smoke. Again, he asked one word: 'English?'

'Yes,' said Doyle, and added incongruously, 'Middlesbrough, Yorkshire.'

The headman nodded as though he might have expected as much, and indicated with a gesture that Doyle should also sit down. Doyle did so, crossing his legs painfully in the fashion of the others.

Through slits and gaps in the floor and the wooden walls, he could see the village; no children, no women. The place appeared deserted. Had they all fled? Surely not. This was their country, after all. They were not Indian traders, or British families, they were Burmese.

The stairs creaked. A man came up carrying a beaten brass tray with some cups of tea without milk or sugar. Leaves floated on the black steaming liquid. Doyle was handed a cup. He sipped it, for the tea was too hot to drink quickly. It tasted strongly of woodsmoke.

'I'm on the way north,' he said, for something to say. He could not understand why he had been invited here, but although they appeared friendly, he felt insecure. Had he walked into some kind of trap? He remembered the Burmese at Henzada and his disquiet increased.

More creaks from the outside stairs. This time the doorway was darkened by four men, much younger and stronger than his host and his companions.

Doyle saw with concern that one wore the saffron robes and had the shaven head of a *pongyi*. He remembered a man similarly garbed outside Henzada waving the marines on to their death. Doyle stood up, partly to greet the newcomers as an act of courtesy, and partly because he realized he was now hopelessly outnumbered. Yet why should he feel danger? They had offered him courtesy and hospitality but some inner instinct beat warning drums in his brain and blood.

As he stood up, the four newcomers, whose hands had been in the folds of their *longyis*, now removed them. Each man held a sharpened dah. Their hostility was obvious. They were going to attack him, maybe kill him. But why?

Words choked in Doyle's throat. His chest felt as if it would burst. He could say nothing, he could hardly breathe, and yet, and yet, he was not going to die.

'You English,' said the headman, his voice different from when he had first spoken, now harsh, bitter, contemptuous. 'You are running away.'

'We will come back,' Doyle answered him, finding his voice. The man sneered and spat on the floorboards. From the corner of his eye Doyle could see one of the young men take half a step forward.

Doyle began to back away towards the stairs. No one moved. Then the nearest man lunged at him with his dah. Doyle jumped back through the doorway and raced down the stairs. He did not stop until he had reached the track. He drew his revolver from his belt and ran with all the speed he could command. Such was his despair that he did not feel the pain in his wounds, until finally he had to stop from exhaustion.

Heart pounding, he crouched down, as he had seen runners after a race lower their heads, and listened. No one was following him. He had escaped this time, but would there be another? He was an obvious target. There must be villages he could not see or even imagine on either side of the track. News of refugees was probably being passed from one village to another, from one settlement to another. A man on his own, especially an Englishman on his own, was sport for those who savoured the chase and the kill. Doyle pushed his revolver back into his belt and trudged on steadily.

Days followed nights followed days...

Within the week he experienced another example of Burmese attitudes towards refugees who they considered to be weak and defenceless.

In abandoning homes, livelihoods, sometimes even their families, and usually their possessions and life savings, it was as though refugees had also lost their personalities. They were no longer individuals capable of initiative on their own. When one stopped, they would all stop and look about fearfully. Some would sit down, heads in their hands, hope gone, courage vanished away.

On this particular day Doyle saw two people who proved the exception to this: a young Indian and his wife, both in their early twenties. With them they had their son, possibly two years old. The mother carried the boy on her hip. She wore a blue sari edged with gold, now dusty and stained from weeks on the road. Round her neck she wore three fine gold necklaces and gold bangles on each wrist. On the side of her nose she had two tiny gold stars. It was the custom for many Indian women to buy gold ornaments; they preferred this to keeping their money in a bank.

Her husband had not shaved for days, and his eyes were red and raw from dust and the sun. He explained that he had been a clerk in a mercantile company in Prome. Somewhere he had lost his spectacles and, without them, he could only see men as trees walking and trees as vague shapes.

Doyle was attracted to them and the feeling was mutual. They walked for a day together and that night lay down side by side off the track in the jungle.

Next morning the Indian awoke Doyle early.

'We must go on,' he announced. 'It is easier to walk before the sun gets too hot.'

'I need to dress my feet first,' said Doyle. 'You can see what they're like. Then I'll be ready.'

The Indian looked embarrassed.

That is what I mean,' he said. 'You have been kind to us, but our child is not well. My wife said he has a fever, his stomach is upset. You did not hear my wife up with him so many times during the night?'

Doyle shook his head. He had heard nothing from the moment he lay down. He had slept the deep uninterrupted slumber of total exhaustion.

'We must go as fast as we can,' the man continued nervously. 'It may be dysentery or something worse. Typhoid, perhaps.'

'I wish I could help you,' said Doyle.

'We'll help ourselves best if we go ahead.'

Doyle nodded. He understood. The man was being polite. The child might be ill or he might not be ill, but understandably what concerned the father was that they could travel more quickly on their own without an Englishman hobbling along, feet wrapped in rags. Doyle shook hands with them, patted the little boy on the head and watched them go. He felt oddly disconsolate now that he was on his own. He hated the jungle. It seemed to be crawling with people he could not see, a forest of eyes, watching him. He was acutely conscious of being alone.

He set about his daily task of unbandaging his wounds and rebandaging them. There was no water to wash them, and he replaced the bandages, front to back, hoping that the ends were cleaner than the pus-soaked section close to the wounds. It must have been an hour after the Indians left before he was ready to move.

Three miles up the road Doyle caught up with them. They were not marching. They were all lying, faces down in the dust. The man's head had been smashed by something heavy, possibly a pole. The woman lay with one arm still protectively around the body of her son. He had also been bludgeoned to death and her throat was cut.

Doyle knelt down beside them, nauseated at this discovery.

The man's pockets had been turned out and the woman's bodice ripped open and her necklaces and bangles removed. Even the little gold ornaments she wore in her nostrils had gone. Three lives taken for a

163

price of a few rupees, he thought bitterly.

What kind of people were these Burmese who he and his comrades had been attempting to defend?

It was clear that many wanted to be rid of the British, and to this end they welcomed the Japanese. But how long would it take before they realized that in a political vacuum crimes like these would flourish – and without the rule of law, chaos could only increase? And in the meantime, how many innocent men, women and children, like these three lying in the dust, greedy flies already buzzing about them, would die needlessly?

Doyle had no idea where the next village might be. There must be another village, of course, or even a town, he reasoned, but when or where? It could be literally only yards inside the jungle from this track and he might never see it, never hear anyone in it, never even know it was there. The jungle held many secrets; this could be one of them.

The sun turned the sky to blood and Doyle realized that within minutes all would be dark and then he would be marooned in the vast loneliness of the forest. He broke into a kind of shambling run, as though in the few extra yards he could cover he would find sanctuary, security, shelter. The day began to die, with deceptive slowness at first, and then with a rush so that one minute the afternoon was too hot to be comfortable in his sack and his bandaged feet, and the next minute the air felt chill, with the fingers of an evening wind seeking out the space between the sack and the top of his shorts.

In the deepening darkness he felt that eyes on either side were watching him, silent people were following him. They knew he was alone, that he was one and they were many, and they had all the time in the world to hunt him down. He shook the thought out of his mind. It was ridiculous. He was imagining things, getting nervy. There couldn't be anything in that damned jungle. Or – could there? Why couldn't there be? He asked questions and felt afraid to answer them.

Hyenas began to call and laugh in the distance, and all the small insistent sounds of the jungle after dark grew closer and louder. He heard the chirp and twittering of insects, the tiny squeal of some unknown animal as a larger, faster enemy killed it; and all the while the relentless tuctoo, tuctoo of lizards, the ratchet-sounding creaks of crickets, and the croak of bullfrogs. Frogs. That meant that there must be water fairly near if there were bullfrogs.

Ahead of him and to one side, under the newly risen moon, a great square of phosphorescence suddenly glowed, the size and shape of a tennis court. Green, mysterious, ethereal – what the devil was it? Doyle stopped to stare at this, and then realized it must be a reservoir, what locals in Burma and India called a tank. The greenness was some kind of weed, like cress, which often completely covered these tanks. He had heard of soldiers coming back to their quarters, after a heavy night in the canteen, and attempting to walk across them, under the impression it was a lawn. With a tank of this size, surely there must have been buildings, huts, where people had lived or worked or pumped water?

He quickened his pace in the darkness, hands outstretched in case he walked into a tree. Fifty yards on, against the reflection of the moon on the waterweeds, he saw a dark square in silhouette; a stone building. He approached this cautiously and stopped outside the door, listening. Nothing. He took a step forward. The door was jammed open or had rotted away. He was not sure which in the darkness. He had no light and could only go cautiously by feel and smell. The smell inside was of diesel oil and grease. He could not smell any animal or human, and there was no sound. He was alone.

He held out both hands in front of him, like a blind man, to feel his way and to sense safety. If he fell down a hole and broke a leg, he could die here on his own, a terrible death. He shuffled his feet carefully across a dusty concrete floor. When his eyes grew accustomed to the almost total gloom, he could make out some kind of dynamo or engine. This was bolted to the concrete and had not been looted. He sat down on the floor with his back against this. Ribs on the circular metal cover of the mechanism dug into his flesh. He felt safer sitting up with his stick across his knees, watching the doorway. Sitting there, he ate the rest of the chapattis, salted with his own sweat.

After a time, when he had almost nodded off to sleep, he realized he could not watch all night, so he climbed over the engine, barking his bare knees on metal bolts and fins that seemed to bristle everywhere. The floor on the other side was thick with dust. He brushed a place for himself and lay down. He had not meant to sleep, but within minutes he had dozed off: he was utterly exhausted.

Doyle awoke suddenly, instantly alert and awake with that sixth sense that comes to all people who have ever been close to violent death, in peace or war. He sat up cautiously, because he instinctively knew it would be dangerous to make any noise. He was not sure whether any tins or pots lay around the engine and he could easily hit them with his stick and give an alarm. But who could be

167

out there? Surely not Japanese?

He stood up. A window without any glass overlooked the tank. The moon was up in the sky now, very bright, very full. To the right of the tank, he could see some people bending down, some on their knees, some crouching. From their clothes and distinctive headgear, they appeared to be Burmese. A fire was burning, perhaps to cook an evening meal, but more likely toward off evil spirits, the *nats* which Burmese feared. *Nats* lived everywhere. Some were helpful and some were evil and they never could be certain which kind might be in the vicinity.

A dog barked somewhere; he must be nearer to a village than he'd imagined, and again he heard the cry and laugh and chuckle of hyenas. He stared at the group, trying to make out what they were doing.

Now he saw bodies lying on the ground. He had not noticed them before: perhaps the moon had not been bright enough. They were presumably refugees, little more than bundles of rags. Were they wounded? Were they dead? He had to know, and it was equally imperative for his own safety that he was not discovered. Perhaps they had also been attracted to the supposed safety of this solid building?

He peered closely, but could not make out much more than the movements of those who bent over the bodies on the ground.

Then the moon glinted on something metallic: a pair of pliers. Someone else held a great stone in his hand and deliberately smashed it down. On what? The moon soared above some clouds and Doyle saw what was happening. On the ground lay dead and dying refugees who could go no further. Those who crouched above them with pliers were extracting teeth from their mouths, for what purpose Doyle could only guess. Perhaps a necklace? Perhaps some form of coinage? The significance of the stone being dropped on the faces was what disturbed him most of all. They must be doing this to people not quite dead, to make sure they did die, or at least were stunned before they extracted the teeth. He remembered Dick's remark about Burmese doing this. He had not believed him then. Now he did.

Doyle turned away from the window and sat down. He was trembling. It only wanted one of these people to come into the hut and discover him and they would show him no mercy. What could he do with his stick against thirty or forty? Could they be the headhunters the priest had mentioned? He had no idea. All he knew was that he must get out and away, before he was trapped in this tiny room with only one doorway. Holding his breath, sweating with concentration, he lifted his legs over the dynamo on to the concrete floor and stood behind the doorway, watching left and right. No one looked towards the hut. They were too occupied with their grisly task.

He waited until a cloud scurried across the face of the moon, and in the brief gloom came out on to the road. He walked fast in the centre, his feet making no sound in the dust. Every now and then he stopped and listened, looking over his shoulder, but he was not followed. Now he no longer had the sensation that other eyes were watching him, although from time to time he saw glints of jade in the forest and knew that a Burmese wildcat, or perhaps – please God, not – a tiger must be in there. Whatever they were, they did not harm him. He realized now that the greatest danger to him would not come from four-footed beings, but from those who walked upright on two feet.

He kept on marching, stopping when he guessed he must have covered another 50 minutes of distance, and sitting down by the roadside. The blood pounded in his ears, and his heart thundered in his chest with weariness and hunger, but he drove himself on relentlessly, desperate to put as much space between him and the men around the tank as possible. They were fit and knew the countryside. They could catch up with him easily and, if they realized he was on his own, there would be only one outcome of that chase.

When dawn began to paint thin pink streaks across the sky, he left the road, walked into the jungle for about 20 feet, and lay down. Almost immediately he was asleep.

Unknowingly, he was lying on an anthill, and suddenly ants, half an inch long, reddish and glistening in the sun like rubies, were biting him all over his body. He stood up, cursing, tore off his sack, and rubbed it against his flesh to try to erase them. They dug in their pincers, and though he brushed away hundreds of bodies, they left their pincers in his flesh, a further irritation.

He moved deeper into the jungle and sat on the trunk of a fallen tree; it did not seem safe to lie on the ground. But he must have slept as he sat, because when he awoke the sun had climbed up the sky again and he was lying on his side on the ground, half curled up, in front of the tree. He stood up. His body ached and was raw from the bites of the ants. He had no idea what time it was, no idea where he was, but keeping the sun at roughly the same angle as he imagined it had been the previous day, he retraced his steps to the road.

Doyle had a horror, from stories of explorers he had read as a boy in books borrowed from the junior section of Middlesbrough Public Library, that he might walk round in circles, perhaps only feet from relative safety, but never able to find his bearings.

This time, after nearly an hour, he did strike the track again a bit farther north than where he had left it. At least, he assumed it was to the north. He checked his position with the sun. Had it been over his right shoulder before, or his left? His mind seemed fuddled. He was hungry and thirsty and tired, and could not be certain. What if he was walking south towards the tank and the Burmese again, back into danger? He felt panic rise like a river in his blood, and fought it down. He *must* keep cool. This was no way to behave, to imagine dangers. Enough real hazards existed without inventing them. He remembered almost forgotten training at Stonehouse barracks. To find north, you checked on trees, because any moss grew on the north side. He looked at the nearest trees, but could not see any moss. Then he noticed grey incrustations like dried fungus on one side of a tree trunk. That must be the Burmese equivalent of north. So he was going in the right direction.

That afternoon he caught up with another group of refugees, Europeans and Indians, all carrying their belongings on their backs. He introduced himself.

'Didn't know there were any marines out here,' said the man who appeared to be leading them.

There aren't many. I'm one of the few,'

replied Doyle.

The civilians were keeping too fast and fierce a pace. One man, in his forties, his face like raw meat with his exertions, his shirt soaked with sweat, suddenly collapsed at the side of the road. He writhed in agony, his hands tearing at his chest as though he could gouge a hole through his ribs.

The pain! The pain!' he gasped, and then suddenly his body went limp. The others knelt round him, ripping up his shirt, kneading his chest. The leader felt his pulse and then stood up, shaking his head. Someone made the sign of the cross. Doyle also felt his pulse; there was no beat. The man was dead, presumably of a heart attack.

The others all stood up now and moved away, looking down at someone who only seconds before had been walking with them. It was clear that they wanted to be away as quickly as possible; they did not relish this evidence of their own mortality.

'We can't leave him at the roadside,' said Doyle. 'We'll have to bury him.'

'Our business is with the living,' one of the other men replied. To hell with the dead.'

'Not in my book,' said Doyle. 'The Marines always bury their dead.'

He had nothing to dig a hole with except the end of his stick. He scratched in the dust at the edge of the road. When the others saw him working, they came to help him with walking sticks, bare hands, a knife, a Gurkha's kukri. When they had dug a grave, shallow indeed, but at least a covering for the corpse, they rolled the body into it, and pulled earth over the top. Doyle wondered how long it would be before some animal dug it up. Or perhaps they were all gorged on the thousands of dead bodies that marked the march north?

'Who was he?' asked Doyle. 'Hasn't he a name we could write on a stake of wood?'

'We called him Jock. He was Scots,' one of the men explained. 'He was a box wallah in Rangoon.'

'How d'you mean, a box wallah?'

'It's an Indian description for a trader of some kind. A businessman. In the old days wallahs used to come to the back of people's houses carrying a box on their head full of items they had to sell. When the memsahib wanted to know what they had to show and offer, they put the box on the ground and opened it, and she chose what she wanted. Tablecloths, silverware, anything. I've no idea what his name was.'

So they left him, a man without a name, who in his time had doubtless been a person of consequence, probably with a wife and family already safe over the border. His friends at the club, in his office, on the golf course, would never know what had happened to him, how he had died. Everything for which he had lived and worked was meaningless now: he was an unknown civilian in an unmarked grave by the side of a track leading nowhere. The thought struck Doyle as being immensely sad: a serviceman might expect to die, but death was a risk he had to accept. This man had probably survived the Great War and now, in middle age, death had caught up with him. Doyle recalled the priest's story about the servant with an appointment in Samarra.

'He could have lived,' said Doyle.

'What do you know about it?'

'This. You people, like the last lot I fell in with, are keeping up far too fast a pace. Slow down. Rest for ten minutes every hour. We do that in the Marines and the Army on the march. And we're fit. It's even more important for you than us.'

'You mean that?'

'I *know* that.'

So they moved on at a slower pace. The soles of Doyle's feet had now hardened, toughened. The thin linen strips had again worn through, and he now threw them away and walked barefoot. The wounds in his ankles were still open, still suppurating, and their edges were like yellow lips drawing apart. He had hoped they might heal up and draw together and seal, but the reverse appeared to be happening.

When the sun was directly above them,

they pulled over to one side under the shade of the trees. Their leader glanced at his watch.

'We'll stop here for lunch,' he announced. 'If you can call it that.'

His companions heaved their packs off their backs and sat down thankfully. The weight of their belongings had rubbed through their sweaty shirts to the flesh. One man pulled out a silver flask from his pack, opened it, and sniffed appreciatively at the contents before he put the flask to his lips.

'If you drink that in this heat, you're mad,' Doyle told him shortly.

'Who the hell are you?'

'Someone who doesn't want to see you die like that other man back there.'

'Why should I die drinking this? Never used to drink in the old days before the sun went down, agreed. But dammit, that's all gone now. Gives me a bit of pep, this. Anyhow, there's hardly any left.'

'You won't be left too long yourself in this heat. We'll be burying you next.'

'You kidding, or just being bloody rude?'

'Neither. Just predicting.'

The man looked again at the flask, put it to his lips, and sipped. Suddenly he snapped the stopper back on the flask.

'You're right,' he said. 'I've been having a nip every day on the trek around lunchtime, and I feel like death afterwards.'

'Keep it,' advised Doyle. 'You may need it in a real emergency.'

Someone else had produced two tins of baked beans. He opened one tin with his penknife, and began to spoon out the contents greedily. Doyle's stomach knotted with longing at the sight of food.

'Why not share it around?' he suggested.

'Meaning you want some,' the man replied sourly. 'What have you got to share around in return? Why didn't you bring your own bloody food? I've carried this all the way up from Prome. Why are you walking around in a sack as a shirt? Who the hell are you, anyhow?'

'I've told you, a marine.'

'So you say. But what bloody rank? A sergeant? An officer, a captain, a major?'

'Rank doesn't matter too much now,' said Doyle. 'It's knowledge that will get us through this. Right, you people made a lot of money in peacetime, which I didn't. But you've never been in a situation where you've got to live by your wits, by your knowledge. I have. I can trade knowledge – what I've learned – for food.'

'Like what have you learned?'

'First, how to stay alive. The most important lesson – how to survive; said Doyle. 'How to march only 50 minutes in each hour. And when you rest up, instead of sitting here as though you're enjoying a picnic on the beach, to put out scouts to watch, in case we're attacked.'

'By whom?'

Doyle told them about his experience at the tank. They looked at him incredulously.

'I never met any Burmese,' one of them admitted. 'Except my servants. And they didn't count, really.'

'I'd never met any, either. Not socially, that is,' said Doyle, remembering the silent crowd waiting on the river bank while the firing party shot the three Indians.

'And I'm not too keen on meeting them now. I'd like notice of their arrival.'

'I see your point,' agreed the man. 'Here, have a bite.'

He handed over the tin and the penknife. Doyle ate two mouthfuls from the blade and handed back the tin.

They set off again. That afternoon they found a field of sugar cane and tore up the canes and chewed them desperately until, gorged with sweetness, they sat retching with hunger and yet unable to eat any more of the only food they could find, the cane.

Next morning the group decided to rest. The straps of their packs had eaten into their soft flesh. Swarms of flies followed them, settling on the raw bloodstained patches on their shoulders. Also, the sugar cane had upset their stomachs. They had been up throughout the night, vomiting and with diarrhoea. They felt too ill to go on. Doyle tried to make them change their minds. The longer they stayed, lulled by the false sense of security that they must be miles ahead of the nearest Japanese, the more difficult it would become to leave. Inertia, the creeping paralysis of the East, could overcome them; a man who lay down was infinitely more reluctant to continue than the person who had not lain down at all.

In the main the refugees agreed with him, but still they refused to march on. Let him go on ahead and they would catch him up. So Doyle agreed, hoping to shame them into action, and went off on his own. He walked at a deliberately slow pace, to give them every chance to overtake him. But, by late afternoon, when it became clear that this was unlikely to happen, he quickened his pace. He never saw any of them again.

Days and nights now began to assume an extraordinary quality of timelessness. He felt so tired that he did not bother to look for a hut or a safe refuge at nightfall, but just lay down on the ground, off the track. Mosquitoes buzzed and whined around his face and knees and hands. He would wake up early next morning, his face puffy from their bites, with little specks of blood on his wrists and the backs of his hands.

Once, towards mid-afternoon, he came into a small town, deserted now, the main street littered with items looters had failed to carry away. It had a single-line railway station, but the English language sign had been torn down and he could not understand the Burmese vernacular with all its squiggles and curlicues. He climbed onto the platform, searched the first- and second-class waiting rooms and the refreshment room, hoping that perhaps the looters had left a knife, a fork, or a cup he could steal. Everything had gone; looters were like locusts, he thought, leaving nothing anyone could carry away.

He walked out along the small platform. Behind it, in a siding, stood three trucks. Two were open, the third closed. It was just possible that might contain something he could use; even a pail he could carry to draw water.

The wooden trucks were painted brown, now dried and powdered by the heat of unnumbered summers. The double door had a big swing-over bar that fitted into a slot. He heaved at this, but the bar stayed firm. Cursing, all his bitterness at being left on his own without food or weapons suddenly focused on this bar. For the moment it did not matter what the truck contained, whether indeed it contained anything at all. The important thing was to open it, to prove he was not a total loser.

For a second the bar still resisted him, then

unexpectedly it dropped. He pulled open one of the two doors. From inside the truck jumped a man holding a machine-gun. He jammed its muzzle against Doyle's naked navel, forcing him back across the track.

He was a small wiry man wearing the remnants of a khaki uniform that looked vaguely familiar. He had a smooth face, a flat nose and the slit eyes of a Japanese – or could he be Chinese? That was it, he must be from a unit of the Chinese army.

Doyle stood, staring at him in shocked amazement. His heart beat like a drum, as he raised his hands in the universal signal of surrender. The man shouted something at him angrily in a language Doyle did not comprehend. Doyle shook his head.

'English,' he said hoarsely. 'English!'

The man nodded as though he dimly understood the word. Slowly he lowered the muzzle of the gun.

'Food,' said Doyle, and pointed a finger at his own mouth and tapped his stomach. The man shook his head. Behind him now in the gloom, Doyle could see several frightened faces. The truck was full of young women. They wore drab uniforms, shirts and loose trousers. Seeing the amazement on Doyle's face, they started to giggle. Doyle shook his head.

'Food,' he repeated, and patted his stomach again. The other nodded, and shook his head in reply; he had no food. That much was clear.

Doyle guessed that he was in charge of the women, known euphemistically as 'comfort girls', for the Chinese army. But where was the Chinese army, and why should a dozen girls and one armed Chinese soldier be locked up in a truck abandoned in a siding where no train would arrive for months? To answer this question was not Doyle's most immediate concern. He wanted to survive, and this fellow could be trigger-happy. Doyle shrugged, held out one hand. The Chinese soldier took it. They shook hands solemnly.

Doyle turned and walked back through the station towards the track. As he walked, he found he was tensing his back muscles, as men who have been under fire tend to do when they walk away from danger. This was a totally reflex action, as though by tightening the muscles he could provide a shield to deflect any bullet aimed at him. The idea was fanciful and absurd, and he realized it and consciously relaxed the muscles. Then he looked over his shoulder. The Chinese soldier was still looking after him. Doyle waved. The man made no movement. Doyle walked on. He came out of the station and thankfully reached the track.

Several miles up the road, when he was beginning to wonder where he would find a place to bed down at dusk, Doyle saw something sticking out of the foliage. He came closer, and then stood looking at a pair of shoes worn down at the heel with holes in the soles. He lifted branches that concealed the body of a man. He must have died quite recently, because the corpse had not yet started to putrefy. A handful of greedy flies had gathered at the mouth and nostrils. Doyle wondered how he had died, what had killed him. A stroke? Hunger – or simply because he had lost the will to survive?

Doyle was about to lower the branch and go on his way when he saw a lanyard around the man's shoulder. Underneath the corpse was jammed an Army issue metal water-bottle in its khaki cloth case. Doyle pulled the lanyard free and dragged out the bottle. It was full. He removed the stopper and drank greedily. The water revived him. He slung the lanyard over his shoulder and went on more cheerfully With water he could survive, and now he could fill the bottle at every stream he saw. The lanyard had frayed rotten with sweat around the buckle and where it fitted the bottle, and was clearly not the original webbing issue; someone had cobbled up a replacement in a hurry.

He passed little groups of refugees who were lying exhausted under what shelter the trees could give them. Some were obviously ill, suffering from heat stroke, dehydrated, eyes shut, mouths open, gasping for breath, with white salt forming a telltale rim around their cracked, dry lips. Others, too weary or ill to move, sat with their backs against the trunks of trees, heads forward on their shoulders between consciousness and oblivion. They were too far gone to notice him; already they were all but dead.

Beyond the track he saw an Indian sitting, back against a tree, mouth moving as though trying to speak, but no sound came out. His eyes opened as Doyle approached. They were bright with fever. Doyle paused, looking at him, wondering whether he could help him. The man stank of sweat and excrement and vomit. He was also dying by degrees; it was doubtful whether he would last till the end of the day.

The Indian raised a finger, dry and shrivelled as a bird's claw, and pointed to the bottle. His lips moved in the motion of swallowing. In his fever and delirium, he was already drinking long cool draughts of fresh water. Doyle held out the bottle towards him, and then pulled it away. It would be madness to give it to this man; he'd be dead within hours, probably minutes. A last drink could not possibly save anyone in his condition. Also it might not be safe to drink from the rim after his scummy cracked lips had been around it. Doyle slung the bottle back on his shoulder and went on. Behind him he heard a pitiful cry, thin and weak, as a tiny animal might give when snared in a trap.

Doyle did not look back, but several times he paused. The image of the Indian dying alone, a man to whom he had refused even a mouthful of water, disturbed him. He felt mean, selfish, and hated himself. Then he rationalized. That old Indian was probably dead by now. And did it really matter either way? In all the thousands who must have died in Burma so far, and millions who had died in the war, in Germany, in France, in North Africa, in Italy, in Russia, the Pacific, on land, in the air, on the seas, beneath the seas, did one more death count for much? Of course it did, to the man who died, to his family, his friends. And I refused to help him, he thought. I could have done *something;* a drink of water was little enough, but I didn't even give him that.

He was walking head down, turning this over in his mind. With hunger and weariness, his thoughts took on a curious clarity. He could only think of one thing at a time, and even this was better to think about than the possible outcome of this barefoot trek. Suddenly he paused. He had felt a strange trembling through the soles of his feet. Something large was coming towards him, beyond the bend of the track which he could not see. He crouched, ready to run into the jungle on either side.

A huge boar thundered into view, head down, curved tusks pointing towards him. He must have been frightened or disturbed. Doyle jumped into the bush. Creepers tripped him and tore at him. Thorns lacerated his flesh, but he did not feel their sharpness, or the razor edges of leaves. He had to escape from this pounding animal, perhaps a ton of flesh and muscle, bone and sinew and tusks. The beast raced on past him, out of sight.

Doyle stayed where he was, panting with exhaustion and shock and reaction. He could have been gored, killed, left to die. God, was there no end to the horrors of this jungle?

He waited until he thought the beast must be half a mile down the track, and then, very cautiously, he came out. He paused, listening in case it returned. Only then did he start off again in the direction he had been walking.

His mouth felt as dry as a hot bread oven. He put his hand down to swing the bottle up to his lips. Nothing. He patted his chest, his body, in case the bottle had slipped around, out of sight, but it was not there. The frayed lanyard must have caught on some branch as he dashed into the jungle. It was rotten, in any case, and had snapped and the water-bottle was lost with all the water it contained. He would have been wiser to have given the whole bottle to the Indian. The irony of the situation, the aptness of what he felt was poetic justice, made him laugh. Suddenly he started to roar with laughter, as though the whole incident was the greatest joke he had ever heard, the funniest experience of his life. And then he stopped, and the echo of his laughter seemed to beat back from the trees. Or was it all an illusion? Was he going mad? He pressed the palms of his hands into his aching eyes, and even through the thickness of his hands, it was as though he saw the sun pulsing, beating, burning, with a heart of its own, a furnace in the sky. He went on more slowly until he found a place where he could curl up and sleep.

Later, days later, in the upper room of an otherwise empty house which he entered in the hope of finding a knife or a spoon or a mug, he saw a broken hand mirror, dropped when looters had fled. He picked up a sliver of glass and looked at the reflection of his face. He could not recognize himself; his skin was almost black, hair long, and a beard growing unkempt and straggled. From walking into the sun, his eyes had sunk deeply into his head; they were bloodshot and yellow.

Everything that could be carried away, or broken for firewood, or to make another hut or a shelter from the coming monsoon, had been stolen from the house. However, there was still a bucket suspended in a primitive well, and he drew this up, threw out the old water, refilled the bucket from the well, and, ripping his clothes off, poured the contents of bucket after bucket of cold water over himself. Then he washed the sack and his shorts as best he could, wrung them out, and used the sack as a towel to dry himself.

At the back of the house he saw a small cultivated patch. While his shorts and sack dried on the verandah rail, he walked through this, naked as Adam, searching for any vegetables he could grout up. He saw some withered leaves yellowing in the sun, but he was not sure what they were. He broke a piece of wood off a loose plank, and using this as a spade, he dug out a long pinkish tuber like a potato. He forced himself to swallow the cold, almost indigestible mass – and then he heard a familiar noise he had not heard for months: the clucking of chickens.

Two or three chickens, thin, scrawny, with feathers pecked out, came through the bushes and stood looking at him. They must have thought it was their owner coming back to feed them. He threw them half of the potato he was eating. They pecked at it listlessly and went back into the bushes. He followed them carefully, intending to catch one and eat it raw. Sensing danger, they kept out of his way. Then, in a nest of leaves, he saw two very small brown eggs. He picked them up. They were still warm, whether from the hen or the sun he did not know and did not care, nor did it matter. They represented food.

He was about to bite into the shells and eat them raw, but somehow, after the raw potato, hungry as he was, the idea repelled him. He searched around the edge of the patch in case he could find anything else to eat. There was nothing. Then the sun winked on bright metal: a pair of old steel-rimmed spectacles that had been thrown away. One lens had disappeared, the other was badly cracked. He picked it up and put it to his eye. The magnification was enormous. Whoever had used these spectacles must have been almost blind.

He was about to throw them away when he realized that the cracked lens could be used as a burning glass. He went back into the house and found half a sheet of old newspaper with peculiar Burmese script, all circles and squiggles. He carried this out, squatted down behind the house, tore the paper into small pieces, and picked up a few twigs and laid them across it. Then, holding the spectacle lens in his hand, he moved it nearer and then farther away from the paper until he focused the sun as a small point of brilliant light. It was so bright that his eyes ached and watered.

Slowly the paper grew warm. A wisp of smoke fluttered from it, and then it took flame. Within minutes, he had a fire. He put a little water in the bucket, balanced this on three stones over the fire, put the eggs in the water, and waited until they boiled. He poured out the water, picked the eggs from the bucket, shelled them and ate them. Now he boiled the sweet potatoes until their reddish skin peeled off. He devoured these wolfishly. The warm food cheered him up immensely.

He broke the lens off the bridge of the spectacles, wrapped it in another piece of paper to protect it, and also to have some kindling paper when he wanted to light another fire. Then he put the lens and the paper into the back pocket of his shorts, and set off again up the road. As he did so, rain began to fall, a patter-patter of raindrops on the flat fleshy leaves all around him, faint as the beat of distant drums. Then the heavens opened and a solid wall of water cascaded out of the sky.

The monsoon had begun.

As the padre who left the train and the priest in Myitkyina had warned him, everything changed immediately. Doyle had accepted that the monsoon would mean heavy, even continuous rain, but this was not rain as he had ever seen it. This was a deluge that swamped the land, a third dimension he had neither envisaged nor imagined. He was walking in the centre of a cataract; it was as though Niagara stretched across an entire country. He knew that apart from any momentary shelter he might be fortunate to find in an abandoned house, there was no escape from this pitiless, driving rain. He could be soaking wet for months.

Soon his throat swelled and he found difficulty in swallowing. He chewed leaves, stalks, anything to try and ease the pain and constriction. His sack and shorts stuck to his body like a second, rotting skin. Leeches also clung to his flesh, and when he tore them off, thick and soft and foul, they squirted blood, his blood. He walked in water; he crouched by the side of the track to rest in water; he lay down to try and sleep at night in water. And when he awoke there was no release, no reprieve.

The constant downpour obliterated most other sounds, but sometimes it slackened, and in those brief periods, Doyle gradually became aware of a larger roaring of water in the distance. The sound grew louder as he approached, and finally the jungle parted and the track petered out on the edge of a ravine.

Far beneath him, a river surged in a boiling, foaming, fuming fury. Trees, branches, the bodies of dead animals were carried on its flood like weightless toys. Above this torrent hung a thick white mist of spray. On the far side, perhaps seventy or eighty feet away, he could see a sheer cliff and then the jungle, always the jungle, thick, green, hostile, stretching into infinity.

He sat down wearily on the edge of the forest, his back against some unknown tree and stared in disbelief at the flood, trying to work out a way to cross it. If he climbed down one side, he knew he would be unable to brave the force of that current, and the cliff on the other side was in any event unclimbable.

The monsoon had ripped away shrubs and climbing plants that might otherwise have provided him with handholds or footholds. It seemed inconceivable that he could have come so far and then be faced by this insurmountable obstacle. He tried to force himself to think more positively. It *was* inconceivable. The track had led here and would not therefore end here; so there must be a way across. *There must be* – and he would never find it sitting where he was.

Doyle stood up, shook rain from his hair, and began to walk along the edge of the ravine.

Mud had splattered the undergrowth, which meant that other people had been here before him. Animals would never leave such a wide and obvious track. Sure enough, about a mile ahead, he saw a little group sheltering beneath the trees. They were women and children, Indians and Europeans. Some stood, others crouched on their haunches. One or two, obviously far gone with fever, had thrown themselves down on the ground and lay, oblivious to the driving spears of rain and the immensity of their misery.

Because of the roar of the river, they did not hear Doyle approach until he was within feet of them. Then one woman, standing a little apart from the rest, turned and faced him. She wore a shapeless dress of some cotton material. Her dark hair hung around her shoulders, streaming with water. She had well-cut features and in any other circumstances would have been pretty. Her face was so burned by the sun that she could have been English or Anglo-Indian or even Indian. With women who had lived for a long time in the East, it was sometimes difficult to tell their nationality until they spoke. She had the air of a governess or a housekeeper. She was clearly trying to put on the bravest face, but Doyle guessed she was probably terrified.

'Who are you?' she asked him coldly.

He knew then from the Welsh lilt of her voice that she was Anglo-Indian.

'I'm a Royal Marine,' Doyle replied. 'Have you been here long?'

It seemed like one of those absurd openings to a conversation between a couple introducing themselves in a dance hall: 'Do you come here often?'

'A day and a half,' she replied.

'Is there a way over?'

'Yes. A ropeway. We can cross one at a time. Upstream.'

'What's the matter, then? Is it cut?'

'No.'

Then why haven't you used it?'

Doyle was standing close to her now, and could see the lines of exhaustion etched in her face. She was probably no more than 30, but she looked twice her age.

'For two reasons. First, there are two armed natives standing on the other side, waiting for us.'

'Natives? What do you mean? Burmese, Indians?'

'I don't know,' she admitted. 'I've never seen men like them and I've lived in Burma all my life. They are naked, except for some cloth around their middle, and they carry huge knives like dahs in their hands, and they're just standing there. They could cut anyone down as soon as they reached them.'

'I see,' said Doyle. This seemed justification enough to delay the crossing.

'What's the other reason?' he asked.

'A British officer came through here yesterday,' she explained. 'He didn't cross there himself, but he went further up. He believed there was a second ropeway, and then he'd come back and fetch us.'

'Did he find one?'

'I don't know. He told us to wait here for him. He said he would be back.'

'But you can't wait here indefinitely,' Doyle pointed out. 'If I cross, will you follow?'

'But what about the officer? We gave our word we'd wait for him.'

'You could wait just as well on the other side. No doubt he means to come back, and he will if he can. But we don't know what has happened to him. And you owe it to yourselves to cross while you can. He'll understand.'

She looked at him, thankfulness showing on her face. 'You think so?'

'I'm certain,' Doyle declared stoutly.

He did not like her description of the two men guarding the far crossing. Could these be headhunters the padre had mentioned?

There was only one way to find out. He went into the trees, turned his back to the little group so they would not see him and swung his revolver round to the front of his body. He broke it. Water was in the chambers. He peered through the barrel; it was furred with rust. Two shots, two men. He could not afford to miss, and yet it could be madness to fire before they attacked, because they could be guards or scouts for a much larger group or colony. He would not use the revolver, would not even let anyone see it, but the knowledge that he possessed it gave him comfort of a kind. And, he thought grimly, it was the only comfort he had. He replaced the revolver beneath his belt, turned to face the group.

'When you're ready, I'm ready,' he said simply.

They set off in single file. The well helped the ill. Doyle carried a little boy on his shoulders, piggyback, as his father used to carry him to a football match when he was too small to see over the heads of those in front; a different time, a different world.

They reached the rope bridge. Two ropes had been lashed to the trunks of trees on each side of the ravine. In between, bamboos were woven into the ropes, like the rungs in a ladder. About three feet up on either side stretched two other ropes, to give a handhold for those who could not bear to walk upright, or felt unable to crawl on hands and knees without such support. Doyle could see no one on the far side. He turned to the group.

'I'll go over first,' he told them. 'Just to see everything's all right. Then I'll wait and you'll follow. Whatever you do, don't look down or up, but always straight ahead, otherwise you may lose your balance.'

The woman in the cotton dress translated in case the Indians in the party did not fully understand what Doyle had said. They nodded their heads. A little girl began to cry. Doyle ruffled her hair.

'You'll be all right,' he assured everyone. 'Keep close, one behind the other. Don't straggle. Be like a long serpent going across, a school crocodile, if you like. You understand?'

'We understand,' said the woman. 'Is there anything we can do to help?'

'Pray,' said Doyle, only half jocularly.

'We will do that, all of us, silently.'

Doyle turned towards the bridge, put one foot on the nearest rung. The whole contraption swayed alarmingly from side to side as the rung dipped with his weight. The loose guide ropes on either side swung up above his shoulders. It would be impossible for any small person to cross holding onto them because the weight of others behind or in front of them would pull the bridge down even further. He would have to lead by example, showing them the only way they could safely attempt the crossing: on their hands and knees.

Doyle began to crawl, a rung at a time. Sharp splinters of bamboo cut his hands and his knees, but he barely noticed the lacerations. He moved slowly, carefully, his eyes fixed constantly on the far side. He knew that if he looked down, he would feel giddy, and once that happened, he was lost.

The bridge dipped sharply as he reached the centre, and then suddenly the angle changed and he was climbing steeply. He had crossed the halfway mark.

He paused to regain his breath. Rain beat down, blinding him. Only feet below, the river thundered, and spray soaked him. He shook water from his eyes and noticed a slight movement on the cliff top. He tried to convince himself that this must only be the branches of trees, trembling in the wind. Then he saw two men, just as the woman had described, watching him.

They were partly shielded by the foliage, but as they realized he had seen them, they stepped out into the open. They were tall, naked except for reddish loincloths, and in their right hands they held long Burmese dahs. The blades glittered in the streaming rain.

Their appearance was so grotesque, so sinister, so threatening that Doyle felt his stomach knot within him. He paused. Every instinct cried for him to retreat. But that was impossible now. He had come too far to go back; he had to go on.

He gave a vague nod in their direction to show that he had seen them, and began to move ahead slowly, rung by rung. The angle of the ladder increased steeply. Twenty more steps to go; fifteen; ten; six, and he reached the bank.

He stood up carefully, holding his hands, palms open towards them, to show he had no weapon. The two men glanced at him, but did not acknowledge his presence by so much as a nod of their heads. They continued to stare back across the ravine; he might not even have been there. What were they watching? Who were they expecting? For the moment that did not matter, because they had not offered him violence or hostility. If they were not his friends, at least they were not his enemies. He held out a hand in a gesture of friendship. They still ignored him. He turned and called to the others.

'It's quite safe. Come on over.'

Several of the children looked in terror at the guards, who still paid no attention to any of them. When everyone had crossed the bridge, Doyle shepherded the little party along the track into the jungle. He walked behind them, because he thought that if the two men were going to attack anyone, they would attack him, and he had the revolver. He could imagine his head being chopped off any moment before he could draw it, and instinctively he braced his back muscles against a blow from their dahs, but nothing happened.

He did not dare to turn his head and see

whether they were watching him, or worse, following him, but marched on resolutely behind the women and children. Half a mile along the track he called on them to halt and went to the head of the column.

'Let us give thanks to God,' said the woman in the cotton dress, and knelt down in prayer.

'We will wait here,' she announced, standing up.

'What for?' asked Doyle. 'Come on with me. We can't be much more than a hundred miles from the border. We will take it in easy stages.'

'But the officer,' she said. 'I *promised* him we would wait.'

'He'll understand.'

'I gave my word.' she went on stubbornly. 'He was an English gentleman. His word will be his bond. What will he think of me when he comes back and cannot find us?'

'I beg of you to come,' said Doyle earnestly. 'Something must have happened to him. You cannot wait. You must see that.'

'I do. But I gave him my word.'

Doyle argued with her for twenty minutes, but she remained adamant; she would not go. Doyle then asked the others if they would follow him, but only received a polite shake of their heads – they would wait with their leader. She had brought them so far, safely. She had given her word. It was a matter of honour.

It was a matter of folly, thought Doyle angrily, but since he could not persuade them to accompany him, he walked on by himself in the rain.

At the end of the track, before it twisted deeper into the jungle, he turned. They were standing under the trees, a forlorn little group, just as when he had first seen them. They could have been a still life tableau and not real people.

The woman in the cotton dress waved to him, and for a moment he thought she would follow him. But when he beckoned her to do so, she shook her head.

Pondering on honour and what the word could mean to one person, and because of this interpretation, what it could also mean to the lives of others, Doyle walked on, and the jungle hid them from his view.

Days, nights passed in a kaleidoscope of drenched and dripping images: rain, rain, rain...

Ahead of him, half collapsed across the track, now a streaming torrent of water, Doyle saw the ruins of a wooden house tilted to one side. The stilts that supported it must have given way. As he approached, he realized why. It was not because of the rain, but a bomb appeared to have landed slightly to the north of the building, blowing off its back, cracking its supports. Splinters of wood from the balustrade glistened white in the rain, like bone. Shutters swung from side to side, reminding Doyle of swinging inn signs back in England. To Doyle this house represented shelter, an opportunity to wring out his sack and his shorts, take off his bandages, and even if he found nothing with which to dry himself, at least he could stand naked in a relatively dry place.

It was more difficult than he had imagined to climb up on to the creaking, swaying balustrade, and then to slide down the slope into the main room. Some furniture still remained. A print of the Shwe Dagon pagoda with its golden roof hung precariously off one wall from its nail. On the floor lay a broken plaster Buddha and what looked like sparklers from a fireworks kit. Joss sticks. Perhaps this had been a priest's house?

He saw some letters on the floor and turned them over, not knowing what he was looking for. They were written in Chinese script. He opened a cupboard; sodden clothes fell out. In the back of the cupboard he saw a cardboard shoebox. The lid was saturated with dampness. The box contained a mass of small glass bottles with screw caps and white labels on them – aspirin. He opened one and took three aspirins, but was unable to swallow them because of his swollen throat. He chewed them, holding his hand out under the broken gutter for some rain to wash them down. He put two phials in his pocket. They were no use against malaria, but they might help to fight other fevers and possibly perhaps the almost chronic headache from which he was now suffering.

The room was a disappointment. It was damp and he could not lie down and sleep at an angle of 45 degrees. Also, there was something about the house he disliked – a miasma of death. Looking through a gap in broken floorboards, he saw the cause: two corpses lying half out of the shelter of the house. He climbed down to have a closer look at them. He had seen so many corpses, two more made no difference.

These were not Burmese. Their clothes, although soaked with rain and putrefaction, were dark red pantaloons edged with gold, and a long tunic with loose sleeves. They were probably middle-aged, he guessed, but it was difficult to be certain because their bodies were bloated and blown up with gas. Animals had eaten the head off one man; the other head crawled with worms in the eye sockets. The bitter aspirin reacted on Doyle. He retched, the sight was so disgusting.

Then he saw, a little to one side of the corpses, a lacquered black box of a kind he had often noticed for sale in Indian bazaars. It had a brass handle at each end, with ornate brass hinges and a big brass lock. He tried to open it, but the lock stayed shut. There must be a key somewhere, he thought. If the two men had been carrying this box, as seemed likely, it must contain something valuable – and one of them would have the key.

He looked at the men more closely, then picked up a stick, and hooked the sleeves off their wrists to see whether there was a key. Then he poked the stick at the decomposing mass of flesh that had been a man's neck. Here he saw the glint of gold; a fine necklace. Carefully he slipped the end of the stick under it and gently lifted the stick. Two keys came into view. He tried to loosen them from the necklace, but despite its flimsy delicate appearance, he could not do so. He would have to pull it over the head-less neck of the man.

He could not bear to touch that slimy yellow flesh crawling with worms, as big as fingers. Shutting his eyes, and holding his breath in case he breathed in the filthy smell of decay and decomposition, he gently manoeuvred the necklace over the headless stump. Then he carried it out on the end of the stick into the rain, threw it into a puddle and pulled it to and fro until all the threads of flesh and worms had been washed away. Now he picked up the keys and tried them in the lock. The first would not move, but the second turned easily. The lid sprang open with unexpected force. Then he saw the reason. The box was packed solid with ten-rupee notes, and beneath them, gold coins. He had never seen a gold coin before; he picked them up now, one by one, and examined them.

He was looking at a fortune, more money than he had ever seen in his life, perhaps more than he would ever earn in his life, and all useless. He could not carry it with him. He had no bank in which he could deposit it. There was no point in burying it because he would never find this place again, and somehow the incongruity of so much accumulated wealth in these circumstances nauseated him.

He would have given all of it to be safe, to be dry, his ankles cured, wearing boots, clean clothes, after a shave, with his teeth brushed, his hair combed. A handful of these notes could have bought all of these desirable things – if they were for sale. But they were not on offer. At that moment they had no price: they were priceless.

He let the lid fall down on the money, and he did not even bother to lock the box. But he put the key in his pocket as a memento, something to remind him of a fortune he had found when a fortune was useless.

His mind was now a turmoil of conflicting and futile emotions; regret at leaving the money, irritation at ever having found it. Surely it would have been better to pass by without knowing it was there?

This was no place to linger. He pulled on the soaked garments and then, head down against the rain, grinding his teeth against the pain in his ankles and the bitterness in his mind, he left the house behind him and did not look back.

Doyle heard faint chattering to one side of the track, as of birds, a flock of starlings. He paused. These were not starlings, they were the voices of excited women, talking in a language he did not understand. They sounded troubled, almost hysterical. Gripping his stick, he turned off the track towards them. Five yards into the jungle stood a small hut on stilts, of the type with which he had grown so familiar. A dozen Indian women in saris, soaked with rain, were crouched under the floor. A man stood watching them. He also was Indian, unshaven, wearing a shabby shirt and trousers.

They all looked up as Doyle approached. They were obviously terrified.

'It's all right,' called Doyle reassuringly. 'I'm English.'

The man took a step towards him.

'Who are you?' he asked.

'A Royal Marine. Who are you?'

'A doctor.'

'I heard what seemed like people in trouble,' said Doyle rather lamely as he approached them. On the ground, surrounded by the women, lay a boy of about ten years of age. Someone had thrown a shirt over his body as a kind of covering. He tore at this with his hands. He was obviously delirious. Malaria? Meningitis?

'Is he getting treatment?' Doyle asked the doctor.

'Such as I have.'

The woman nearest to the boy now stood up. She was in her thirties, her face streaked with sweat. She looked haggard, exhausted. Doyle knelt down by the boy, took one of his hands in his. The skin was hot and dry and somehow scaly. He felt the pulse. It trembled and raced as though it had gone mad. He put the back of his hand on the boy's forehead. He was running a very high temperature. Then he remembered the aspirins.

'I've got some aspirins,' he said to the doctor. Would they be any use?'

'In this situation, any medicine is a bonus.'

Doyle turned to the mother.

'Have you a cup, a spoon?'

The woman nodded.

'Give me two spoons.'

She handed him two crudely-made aluminium spoons, stained with food. Doyle held them outside the hut for the rain to wash, then put two aspirins in one of them and crushed them in the rainwater in the bowl of the other spoon. He handed this spoon to the doctor, who held it to the boy's lips. Some of the aspirin mixture went into his mouth, the rest dribbled down his chin. The doctor repeated the dose, this time more successfully, while Doyle crouched by the ill boy, stroking his head, his arms. Gradually he became slightly more calm. Presently he slept, but he was breathing heavily and slowly, as though he had run a long way uphill.

'I'll stay with him,' said Doyle. 'I have some more aspirins when you've used these up.'

There was no need to go on. He might as well stay with these people. At least they were out of the rain and some sort of company, and perhaps he could help the child.

'I've got no money to pay you,' said the woman. 'I must tell you that now.'

'I don't want payment,' Doyle replied. 'We're all in this together. These aspirins didn't cost me anything. They may do no good at all, but, if he gets a chance to sleep, he may improve.'

'I agree,' said the doctor.

Doyle and the mother and the other women took it in turns to stay awake at the boy's side. Twice in the night he gave him more aspirins. In the morning the boy opened his eyes. They were cloudy and bloodshot, but he was much calmer and his temperature had gone down.

The women busied themselves trying to boil water for tea. Doyle held half a cup of the bitter milkless brew to the boy's lips, supporting him with his other hand. He drank greedily.

That day the doctor gave him three more doses of aspirin; he was still not cured, but he was better. The women repaid Doyle's kindness by cooking some vegetables they had rooted up from behind the hut. Doyle had no idea what they were, but he ate them: they were food.

'Are you staying here?' he asked them.

They nodded. 'For the time being.'

'The boy should be able to walk fairly soon,' said the doctor. Then we can move on.'

Doyle took out the second bottle of aspirins and gave it to the mother.

'These will be of more use to you than me.'

Then he stood up; it was time to be on his way.

'Which direction are you going?' the doctor asked him.

'I did not know I had a choice,' replied Doyle.

'You have. The track divides half a mile north. We went up there but could find no shelter, so we returned here.'

'Which way would you advise?' Doyle asked him.

'To the right, without question.'

'Let me borrow your watch a minute,' said Doyle. The doctor unstrapped it from his wrist. Doyle held it in front of him, turned the hour hand to the sun: midway between this hand and the minute hand would be north. If he followed the doctor's advice and took the right-hand fork, he would be heading north-east. He calculated he should go north-west, so he should take the left fork. Doyle explained his reasons for this.

'The right-hand one is the main track: the doctor insisted. 'You will see that more people have gone to the right than to the left. I saw them. I know. And surely it is best to follow where others have been? Is it not written, always follow a known way?'

'I don't know where it's written or who wrote it,' replied Doyle doggedly, 'but the direction's wrong. That way I'll end up in China.'

'China is an ally, is it not?'

'Agreed, but over goodness knows how many mountain ranges. If I keep to the left, at least I will be heading towards India and Assam.'

'I see your point. I can only give you my opinion.'

Doyle was convinced that the doctor was

wrong, and so, when he left the little group, he determined to head north-west, not north-east.

The junction of the two tracks was further away than the doctor had said, or else he was walking more slowly. The afternoon was already all but over when he reached this parting of the ways and paused. Both tracks seemed of roughly equal size, but he unhesitatingly took the left-hand one. After about a hundred yards, it suddenly diminished and then virtually disappeared.

The jungle pressed in on him now from all sides with a physical presence. He pushed ahead vigorously, hoping that this was just a temporary blockage of the way, and that beyond it he would again pick up the track. Great leaves, the size of plates, brushed his face and hands and shoulders. Tendrils like hanging serpents from upper branches dragged themselves against his flesh as he passed. The ground steamed in the heat; he was moving through a rising warm mist. Above his head the branches of trees met, cutting out the sun's rays and the rain. He felt he was walking at the bottom of a sea, deep green all around him, the light filtered by leaves and layers of branches.

Doyle paused and heard an ominous rustle to one side. A snake? A hostile native? Perhaps a headhunter? He had to admit he was walking aimlessly like a blind man. He might even be walking in a circle, as people could do so easily in the jungle when they were lost. He was following his nose, agreed, but in which direction was his nose pointing? He had no means of counting time or measuring distance, and no idea where he was. He was lost.

He stood listening to the rattle of rain on the leaves, and the creak of tree branches against each other, the calls of strange jungle birds, the rustlings on either side and all around him. Was this the end? Was this how he would die, walking endlessly and aimlessly without direction, unable to see the sun by day or the stars at night, until finally fatigue overcame him and he would sink down? Is that how it would be, or would he go mad with the loneliness and this damp cloying warmth?

He shook his head, slapped his face sharply. He must pull himself together. This was no way for a Plymouth marine to think. He turned and looked behind him, to try and establish his position, but suddenly he could not remember whether he had turned a full circle, or just half, or even only a third. Which direction had he been facing? He tried to remember what the trees looked like, but they all looked the same.

Their huge trunks appeared like giant bars imprisoning him. How long had he been standing here? He had no means of measuring time. But now darkness began to fall from the air, like a silent impenetrable shroud. Shadows, which had appeared grey and not unfriendly, were now black and menacing. They might only be shadows, or could they be the entrance to a deep and unknown cave? Leaves had darkened. The sky, which he had glimpsed fitfully through the overhead lattice of branches and fronds as bright blue, now appeared indigo. Within minutes night would enshroud the jungle and he would have to stay where he was, unable to see his way out in any direction, unable to escape any marauding wild beast. For a moment this realization numbed all initiative. But who could help him if he could not help himself? There was no one to guide him, and he could not guide himself. On impulse, in the extremity of his despair, Doyle dropped down on his knees and prayed.

'Oh God,' he said aloud, 'Who has saved me from so many dangers, so many deaths, I beg of You, show me a path, a way forward, if it be Thy will.'

That was the nub of his prayer. But what if the Lord willed otherwise? This thought was so appalling that Doyle tried to drive it from his mind. He could not think of anything more to say, and, still on his knees, he opened his eyes. His face was only a couple of inches from the surface of the jungle. In each direction he could make out small plants and bushes he had not noticed when standing upright. And now he saw something else. To the right of where he knelt, the grass was still trodden and flat; the jungle's soft mossy floor bore imprints of his feet. He had not been able to see this before because, when he was standing up, the leaves and branches of the trees had obscured them. But now, on his knees, he could trace his path.

Keeping on his hands and knees, he began to crawl back along the way he had come. He did not stop until, almost unable to see his hand before his face, he reached the junction of the two tracks. Before he succumbed to the deep sleep of total exhaustion, mental and physical, Doyle knelt down once more and thanked God for his deliverance.

As the days lengthened into weeks, Doyle decided he would have to walk by night as well as throughout each day. Under the light of the rising moon, on the first night he decided to do this, he stepped out as briskly as he could. Then clouds unexpectedly obscured the moon and he was suddenly in almost total darkness. Only the flickering glow of fireflies in the forest gave an eerie uncertain will-o'-the-wisp illumination. They danced and flared and died. Doyle tried to walk on, testing each step by scuffing one foot in the mud. Progress was very slow and gradually he became aware of a great feeling of unease, so strong it was all he could do to force one foot in front of the other. Finally he stopped and crouched down, trying to feel his way with his hands. He moved his fingers carefully to the right; roots and undergrowth. To the left, nothing at all.

He was kneeling on the edge of a precipice. Some basic animal instinct of survival must have warned him it would be death to go on. He lay where he was and waited for dawn. When it came, he saw he had stopped only inches away from a sheer drop of eighty feet.

Doyle walked on grimly. For some time he had heard a roar of rushing water that increased with every step he took, and as he came through the trees, he realized with dismay the size of the river he had to cross. A yellow tide tore past him, bearing branches, sometimes whole trees, and the bloated bodies of cows and dogs, turning over and over, swollen and shining.

Doyle sat down wearily on the trunk of a fallen tree, rain streaming down all around him. He was exhausted, shivering with fever. The thought of trying to swim through that icy filthy water filled him with alarm. He knew he could not make it. He was too tired, too ill. He had marched too far, but he realized now that he had still not marched far enough.

He looked around him desperately, hoping to find some solution to his problem – and was astonished to see thirty or forty other people sheltering beneath the trees nearby. Some were crouching down, as dejected as he felt. Others lay, oblivious to the rain, obviously too ill to care. A few were standing, watching him.

He stood up and walked towards them.

'You speak English?' he asked them.

An Indian, taller than the rest, nodded. 'Yes.'

'How long have you been here?'

'Days, some of us. Others, only a matter of hours.'

'Is there any means of getting across?'

'There was a bridge upstream. But not now.'

'You've been to see it?'

'Yes. It was carried away, or bombed. I don't know which.'

'Well, we can't just stay here,' said Doyle. 'I don't know where the Japs are, but they must be coming up behind us. There's no way around this river?'

Another man, an Anglo-Indian, produced a section of a map, sodden with rain. He pointed with a broken fingernail to a bend in the blue on the map.

'We're here,' he explained. 'We have to

cross somehow, but with this current, we can't.'

'One man could swim it,' Doyle suggested.

'If he were a very good swimmer, perhaps. But what about the rest? My wife and her mother are here with me, and our two children. They couldn't survive the current.'

'Perhaps it will go down when the rain stops,' Doyle suggested hopefully.

'Eventually, in several months' time, when the rain stops, yes. But not until then. Burma has up to two hundred inches of rain in the monsoon, you know.'

'Most of it seems to have fallen on me,' replied Doyle ruefully. 'Are there any wooden buildings around here? Anything we could use as a raft?'

'A raft could not survive. There are some buildings, though. A mill for cutting up teak. It was a big industry here before the war.

'Where are they?'

'Half a mile upstream. There are piles of logs, all waiting to be carted away by elephants. They've gone, of course, with everyone else, everything else.'

'Anything in the buildings we could use?'

'Haven't searched them,' the man admitted. 'Didn't seem any point in it.'

'Well, let's go and have a dekko now.'

The three of them set off along the river bank. The feeling of moving, of doing something, made Doyle forget his own fever, if only temporarily. They reached a cluster of wooden buildings. Huge tree trunks, already shaped and ready for movement, were piled in what had once been a yard and now resembled a shallow lake. They went into the nearest building. A stationary engine, looted of all ancillary parts, stood in one corner. Pages torn from ledgers had been scattered like pieces of damp confetti on the floor.

The second building had been an office, judging from the upturned desks and smashed chairs. In a corner of the third room lay a block and tackle, probably thrown down because it was too clumsy to carry and had no cash value for a looter. Doyle picked it up, surprised at its weight, and carried it out into the yard.

Behind the building he saw a tripod of three huge tree trunks, lashed together at the top. Another block and tackle was suspended from the apex by a long rope. This had been used to lift tree trunks as they could be manoeuvred more easily. The sight of the tripod reminded him of moving old gun barrels by similar means in Fort Cumberland aeons of time ago.

'If we could get one block on the other side of the river, and keep the second block on this bank, and thread a rope through to make an endless belt, people could hang on to it while we winched them across,' he said, really thinking aloud.

'They are both very heavy. How can we get one across the river in full flood?'

'By using a very thin rope or a wire. I could try to swim over with that,' said Doyle. Then I could pull the block across.'

'A thin rope,' said the Indian thoughtfully. 'Let's look.'

They searched in every room of the building, but there was nothing suitable. Then, in an outhouse, Doyle saw a coil of electric wire wound on a drum.

'We'll take that back,' he decided. 'Now, do either of you have a knife?'

The Anglo-Indian nodded and cut down the pulley. Between them they carried the pulleys and rope and the drum of wire back to the refugees. Doyle unwound the wire, tied one end to a tree near the bank and the other around his waist.

'If I get into difficulties in the water, pull me in by this wire. It doesn't matter if you let go, because I've anchored it to the tree.'

'Will you make it?' asked the Indian anxiously.

'We'll soon know,' Doyle replied. 'Now, when I get to the other side, *if* I get there, untie the wire from the tree and tie it securely round the pulley. Keep the rope in the pulley and see that one end is tied to the tree as well. Then, if it gets swept away, we'll

219

not have to start all over again. I can't swim this river twice. It's going to be bad enough swimming it once.'

The Anglo-Indian was already lashing the pulley to the tree. Refugees came out from the shelter of the trees to watch. The prospect of escape had lifted all their spirits.

'When I've pulled the rope over, I'll tie it to a tree,' Doyle explained. Then you send over the strongest two men first. The rest should come two at a time and the three of us can pull them. Tell everyone not to try and move along the rope themselves, in case they lose their grip.'

The Indian translated, and the refugees nodded gravely. This was literally a matter of life or death; their lives, their deaths.

'Wish me luck,' said Doyle and walked down the bank into the river. The excitement of finding the pulleys and working out his scheme had driven thoughts of his own fever from his mind. Now the sharp shock of icy water pounding his soaking, shivering body brought it back. He trembled with ague.

Trying to walk for as long as he could before he risked swimming, with his bare feet slipping and sliding on boulders he could not see, he edged out towards the centre of the river. Within three paces he was totally out of his depth and the current seized him. He struck out first with a breast stroke, then on his back. Then he attempted a crawl.

Thousands of tons of water cascaded over him. He choked, coughed and vomited, and kept on swimming with the frenetic strength of despair. If he did not reach the far bank, he knew he was as good as dead. So were the refugees who anxiously watched his progress.

He swam until he was sobbing with exhaustion; lights flashed in his eyes, blood hammered at his heart. He had no idea whether he was near the bank or still far away; or whether he had been torn away from his original course by the force of the current.

He allowed his feet to drop. They did not touch bottom. He struggled on, and then lowered his feet for a second attempt – and stubbed a toe on a boulder. Choking, gasping for breath, body hunched up to fight the weight of water against him, he toiled towards the shore. As the river grew shallower he fell on his hands and knees to grapple his way up the bank. Then he lay down, panting for breath.

How long he lay he had no means of knowing, but eventually he stood up and walked up the bank, pulling the wire behind him. When he reached the nearest tree, he walked around it three times to wind on the wire, so that if it fell from his hands when he untied the knot it would still not slide back into the river. He made a double knot around the tree and began to pull on the wire. For a few seconds it went slack and then tightened in his hands as the current tugged at the thick rope and the block and tackle. He kept on pulling, slowly, steadily, and finally heaved the block up and out of the river. He made it fast to the tree and pulled on the rope, which the Indian had tied in the form of an endless loop.

The two men on the far bank now went into the river, holding on to the rope with both hands. Doyle pulled with all his strength on one rope, while the others pulled on the other rope round the pulley. Within minutes the two men were safely across. Then followed another man, then a fourth. The five of them kept the rope moving quickly through the pulleys as the women and children began to cross. Mothers tied small children to their bodies with belts or the loose end of the rope. By late afternoon all were across. They left the pulleys and rope where they were; others might need them.

Half a dozen women went on into the forest and cut down bamboo shoots. Doyle produced his broken spectacle lens, but the sun was too watery to start a fire and they had no dry kindling. So they chewed raw bamboos and lay down, hungry and soaking.

By morning the monsoon had briefly abated. The sun was shining. Doyle again produced his lens and this time managed to start a fire with some dry leaves taken from inside a dead and hollow tree. Women chopped up bamboos. One of them produced some rice and a pan, and they ate bamboo shoots and rice, cooking several panfuls until everyone had been fed.

'We will rest up here for a time,' the Indian announced. 'Some of our children cannot walk any further. And we must try to dry our clothes.'

'I will go on then,' said Doyle. 'I cannot wait.'

'You have saved our lives, and we don't even know your name.'

'You probably saved mine,' replied Doyle with a grin. 'So we're quits. If I hadn't been *forced* to do something, we might all still be on the other bank. We owe each other a debt – so they're cancelled out.'

The Indian smiled and shook hands. The little group watched Doyle as he walked out of their lives.

Days, nights passed. He marched, he slept, he ate the food they had given him, and he chewed leaves when that was finished.

Leeches now began to cause him trouble. They were tiny things at first, like minute slugs, barely half an inch long. He could brush them off his bare legs easily enough, but as he walked more and more in water, they fastened themselves onto his knees and calves. Then they swelled to the size of cigars and, bloated with his blood, they would fall off, leaving a scar behind that did not heal. The only way to stop these weeping, raw sores was to burn off the leeches with a cigarette end, but he did not have any cigarettes. They crawled beneath the waistband of his shorts and, when they burst, he was soaked in his own blood that dribbled down his thighs.

Jungle sores on his legs opened into soft wounds that wept sticky fluid. As he walked, the pain from his ankles grew so severe that he coated them with mud, hoping that this might have the same effect as a poultice.

Sometimes a foul odour would give a hundred yards' warning of the carcass of a mule, abandoned by refugees when it died. Vultures, heavy with carrion, would stand in rows on its decomposing body, watching him as he passed. The grim thought crossed Doyle's mind: Did they think he would be providing them with their next meal?

Late one afternoon he came to the edge of another clearing. What in the dry season could not have been much more than a small ravine, perhaps eight or ten paces down to the bottom and then as many more up the other side, was now a raging, roaring yellow torrent. He had to cross it because there was no other way ahead. He felt too weak to attempt the crossing. Also, the hour was late. Darkness would be upon him very soon and it would be madness to attempt such a venture in the dark.

He walked away from the *chaung* for a few yards, seeking any shelter from the rain. He found a bush with huge green leaves the size of dinner plates, and broke off several of these. Lying down on the sodden earth, he tried to cover himself with the leaves, like tiles, to gain some shelter from the pounding rain, but this was futile. He threw them off and lay, soaked by rain, shivering with fever.

He tried to sleep and must have done so, because the next thing he knew was that the sun was shining again and the whole forest steamed. He stood up, thankful for any respite from the rain, and then paused.

Twenty feet away an Indian was sleeping, his back against a tree. He was a plumpish man, probably in his late thirties. He wore linen trousers that had once been white, leather *chaplis* and a tattered shirt, with its tails outside his trousers. To one side of him he had put a white cap, known among the troops as a Gandhi cap, a style much favoured by members of the Congress Party to show their affinity with the Mahatma and his teaching of peaceful non-cooperation with the British as the best way to achieve independence for India. He must have reached the *chaung* as darkness fell, and like Doyle, had been forced to sleep in the open. It was unlikely that he had seen Doyle, or surely he would have made himself known.

Doyle walked towards him. The Indian was suddenly awake, blinking at him nervously. He put a hand into his pocket. For a moment Doyle thought he was going to draw a gun, but instead he took out a spectacle case which contained circular-lensed spectacles with metal rims. He put them on and regarded Doyle.

'Who are you?' he asked him in English.

'A Royal Marine,' said Doyle. 'And you?'

'I am from Rangoon. Now of no fixed abode. A refugee.'

The Indian stood up and Doyle saw that he had been resting against a webbing army pack of the sort soldiers wore on their backs with two loops around their shoulders. The Indian saw him looking at it.

'Just some clothes,' he said nervously and unnecessarily. 'A few things I managed to gather together. Have you any kit?'

'Only what I stand up in.'

'How long have you been here?'

'Came here last night,' said Doyle. 'It was too late to try to cross.'

'I didn't see you. It was too dark. We will

226

cross together?'

'Of course,' Doyle agreed. 'We've a better chance that way. You have a rope in that pack?'

'No, nothing like that. As I said, only clothes.'

The Indian shouldered the pack as he spoke. Doyle could see that it was extremely heavy, dead weight.

'You'll never make it with that on your back,' he said.

'We'll make it together,' the man replied confidently. Two are better than one.'

He put on his cap, folded up his spectacles and replaced them in their spring-back case in his pocket.

'With that pack the current will sweep you away. Why not leave it here? It's not worth risking your life for a change of clothes.'

'No, I will carry it.'

The Indian stepped out into the water and then paused. The water was running, roaring, racing above his knees. Doyle could see that the man could hardly stand upright against its force. He climbed back on to the bank.

'You were right,' he said. 'It is stronger than I thought. Let us go together.'

'Not with that pack,' said Doyle.

He put his hand underneath it; he could barely lift it. 'What the hell have you got in there?'

'Private things. Clothes,' said the man. 'It's no business of yours.'

'Agreed,' said Doyle. 'But it's my business to see I get across, and if you're coming with me, you've got to throw away that pack. *Pegdo* it.'

'Never!'

Doyle gave the pack a slap. It was solid. His fingers had met the hardness of metal. Then he guessed its contents. He took out the key he had removed from the dead Chinaman's neck.

'You got that out of a box this key fits, didn't you?' he asked.

'I don't know what you're talking about.'

'In a house, several days march south. I looked in that box too. And left it there.'

'It's my money,' said the Indian doggedly. 'Nothing to do with that. I also saw that box, open, and like you, I left it where it was. Are we going across?'

'Chuck the pack away first.'

The man shook his head. He gripped Doyle's hand desperately.

'All right; said Doyle reluctantly. 'We'll try. But don't say I haven't warned you.'

He walked into the stream. The water felt curiously warm. His bare feet slipped on large stones, smooth as glass. He edged out carefully into the centre of the *chaung*, bending his body against the force of the current. The Indian had taken off his *chaplis*

228

and held them in one hand, holding tightly on to Doyle with the other. The weight of his pack upset his balance and made him rock to and fro.

The current's very fast,' he said dubiously. 'It will be worse in the middle.'

Another cautious step towards the centre and the water was suddenly much deeper, up to Doyle's waist, and at the same time very cold. The pressure against their bodies was now enormous. Doyle could feel it forcing the breath from his lungs as he went in more deeply. He took a further step forward and almost fell. The Indian was standing, the water up to his armpits.

'I can't go on!' he cried in a panic. 'I can't swim.

'Chuck away that pack!' Doyle shouted above the thunder of the water. 'I can get you over without it.'

The man shook his head. Doyle took another step forward and then lost his balance. He had been bracing himself to pull the Indian along, but the man had let go of his grasp. Doyle was on his own. He lunged after him and caught his shirt. The Indian was screaming now, moving downstream in the current. His eyes were wide and white with terror.

'Your pack! Chuck it away!' shouted Doyle despairingly.

But the Indian was beyond listening, or, if

he heard, he could not summon the will to do what was essential to save his life. He started to stumble, screaming in a high-pitched voice, then turned his back to the current. The linen of his shirt, already rotted by sweat, tore like a sheet of paper and the force of the deluge swept him away downstream. Doyle tried to grab his leg, but the current whirled him out of reach.

Doyle could see the pack, like a khaki hump on the back of some strange water beast, going down the *chaung,* bumping into hidden roots and rocks. He heard the man shouting, until his cries ended in a gurgle. Then there was no sound but the rushing of the water and the rain that suddenly began to fall.

Slowly, inch by inch, Doyle edged his way across the *chaung,* and finally felt the far bank rise beneath his feet. Painfully, wearily, he hauled himself out and lay panting for breath, feeling frozen, yet paradoxically burning with fever, while the water bellowed past him only feet away. He put a hand in his pocket, pulled out the key of the Chinese box and threw it into the stream. For a second the gold glittered in the rain and then it was gone, like the Indian and his pack of stolen money.

Suddenly and unexpectedly the track widened on either side; the jungle appeared to have been cut back. Branches were broken and twisted. In the mud he could see the imprint of heavily-treaded tyres. Trucks had been along here. Trucks? In the jungle? Was he imagining things?

He went forward through the streaming rain, a lean, wiry figure in a sack and rotted shorts, drenched with rain. He felt soft, as though he had been standing for too long under a warm shower. His feet had swollen; they looked like sponges, pocked with small holes where he had cut himself. From these pus oozed. The backs of his hands were black and curiously soft. When he pressed his thumb into his wrist, the imprint remained. He felt he was rotting away.

Every day he had cleaned his teeth, using a piece of bamboo with a jagged edge, but they did not feel clean. He had not shaved since he started and his fingernails were long and broken and cracked. His toenails were soft from walking for so long in mud and water. But despite the almost constant rain, despite the deluge through which he was now walking, his skin burned hot as fire. He knew he was running a high temperature and had been for longer than he cared to remember, but he also knew that the only alternative to march on was to stop, and if he did so he would die.

He put one weary foot after the other, like an automaton, keeping going by his own momentum. When he stopped to rest, he had to force himself to get up. The temptation to lie there, even in the rain, was almost overwhelming, but he instinctively realized that if he did not overcome this yearning, he could lie there forever.

He suffered hallucinations. He could hear people laughing, see the faces of friends from Middlesbrough, from Plymouth, the Maldives, look at him out of the bush, and smile at him, and wave and give him the thumbs-up sign, or two fingers, according to their mood or his. But when he looked again they had gone and the shining spears of rain hammering the great flat leaves of unknown plants emphasized his loneliness and fever.

The track was broadening; there was no doubt of it. The jungle was definitely receding on either side. He saw a turn, twenty yards ahead. I must reach this, there's something important there, he told himself. I must, I *must*. And yet these last few yards – how many paces? – seemed more difficult to cover than all the miles he had walked.

He turned the corner and, to his astonishment, saw a small white tent pitched in an area hacked out of the jungle. It was neatly done. Guy ropes were tight; pegs at the right angle. He stood swaying. Was he imagining this? Was this another mirage, like the faces in the forest?

There was only one way to find out. He

went forward slowly and raised his stick and beat on the roof. The rain had tightened the canvas like a drum. He beat more furiously. Water sprayed all around him, then he saw the flap move at the front of the tent. An Englishman poked out his head.

'I say, old man, no need for all this fuss,' he said reprovingly. 'You'll make it leak if you go on like that.'

Then he saw Doyle and stared at him in astonishment.

'Who the hell are you?' he asked at last.

The man stood up. He was almost as tall as Doyle, wearing a jungle-green uniform, with the three cloth pips of a captain in his epaulettes. He had no hat, so Doyle could not tell his regiment from his badge. He could be in any, or in none. Doyle felt too weary, too ill, to try and solve this problem. He was obviously an officer, or at least he was wearing an officer's uniform, so presumably he should be addressed as one.

'Number Plymouth X100893, Marine Doyle, reporting, sir,' he said. He managed a shaky salute.

The officer looked at him more closely.

'You're absolutely shot with malaria,' he said sympathetically. 'Come into the tent.'

Doyle bent down to enter the tent and collapsed inside, shaking with fever.

'I'm a doctor,' the officer explained.

He gave Doyle some quinine and two

233

tablets that tasted bitter on his tongue. Doyle sat on a canvas stool, holding his head in his hands.

'An orderly and I are an advance medical post, to try and help people who are coming out from Burma. Like you.'

'Have many others come through?' Doyle asked him.

The doctor shook his head.

'You're the first since we've been here. With this rain, you may be the last.'

'Can I stay here?' asked Doyle.

'Sorry, but that's impossible. We've only got what stores a fifteen-hundredweight truck can bring out, and that's all. There's just nowhere to put you up here. You'll have to go on.'

'On, on. I've been going on for months,' said Doyle. 'I came up from Rangoon.'

'Then the rest of the way should not seem so far. There's a construction camp. They'll be able to help you.'

'How far away is it?'

'About ten miles, I'd say. Maybe a bit more.'

Ten miles,' repeated Doyle. 'Can you do anything about my feet, as well as the malaria?'

The doctor examined them.

'I've never seen feet in this condition,' he said slowly.

'Nor have I,' Doyle agreed. 'And they've

done all right by me so far.'

'Can't say you've treated them too well.'

The MO called for a bowl of water, which the orderly brought. He poured in an antiseptic solution and washed Doyle's feet carefully. Then he bound them up with clean bandages.

'What happened to your boots?'

'They went long ago, sir,' Doyle replied.

'I hate sending you on this condition,' said the doctor. 'But there's nothing else I can do. The quinine and the pills I've given you will make you seedy for some time, but they're fighting the malaria. When you reach the railhead, beyond the camp, you will be all right.'

'How far is the railhead?'

'Fifteen, twenty miles, I'd say.'

The orderly made some tea, sweetened it with brown sugar and condensed milk from a tin. Doyle drank it gratefully. The warm liquid made sweat pour out of his body. He had not seen soap for months, and fever and his strange spasmodic diet had altered the scent of his body secretions. He stank.

That night he rested in the tent and then, in the morning, his ankles and feet dressed once more, he set out.

Ten miles up the road (or was it five or eight? He had no idea of distance, no means to count time) he saw several trucks and a bamboo basha. An Indian labour gang was building a road. Women were working steadily, children slung on their hips, as he had seen mothers bring children out of Burma, and at the same time balancing flat wooden trays of stones on their heads. Pioneer Corps soldiers were there with coolies. One had a theodolite; he appeared to be in charge. Doyle approached him. The soldier looked at him with disfavour. Who was this apparition, black of face, bearded, feet bound up like a professional beggar?

'Can I kip the night here?' Doyle asked him.

'It's not exactly a hotel,' said the man shortly. 'Who are you?'

'A Royal Marine.'

'Where from?'

'Rangoon originally. Then Mandalay.'

The soldier grunted.

Well, there's nowhere here except that hut. I'll get you some char, but I'm sorry we have no kit, no fresh clothes we can let you have.'

They went into the hut. Its dirt floor was covered with locally woven matting. There were several bed spaces with cheap rugs or blankets on them. Doyle could not take one of these, so he lay down on the matting, sweating, still soaked with rain, shivering with fever – but at last out of reach of the monsoon.

That night he awoke once and started up,

listening. All around him coolies lay sleeping. The air was heavy with the scent of the oil they used in their hair and on their bodies. One was snoring, another moaned in his sleep, and above their heads the rain drummed with incessant fingers on the bamboo roof.

Were sentries out, Doyle wondered. Was anyone on guard? They could be killed as they lay. And then he realized he was no longer on his own in the jungle; these matters were not his concern. Here he was safe. Thankfully he lay down again on the matting, wiped sweat from his forehead with his forearm, and composed himself to sleep.

Next morning he was offered a breakfast of chapattis and sweet tea, but his stomach was upset by the fever and he could not eat anything. There was no question of dressing. He was already dressed. The rain had stopped momentarily and the ground steamed in bright sunshine. The road looked like a river: mist hung over higher ground like a warm fog.

He saw the soldier he had seen the previous evening.

'Can you give me a lift up the road in a truck?' he asked him.

'Sorry, chum, nothing doing. But it's only about ten miles further on, give or take a bit. Nothing to you if you've walked all through Burma.'

'What is there ten miles further on?' asked Doyle.

'An army hospital. It's been set up for people walking out of Burma. Just tents, you know, but you'll get treatment. Have those feet seen to. They don't look too good to me.'

'They're not. But they've carried me this far. They'll have to carry me on for another ten miles.'

So once more Doyle set off. He thought that it was like following the yellow brick road in The Wizard of Oz, but this time the road had no bricks and was just a yellow river of mud. His legs, despite their dressings, or perhaps because of them, were so painful that he could only limp. But by limping, and resting often, he finally reached the tents. The nearest one had a red cross on a white circle stencilled on the roof. He went into it. The ground was streaming, even beneath the tents, and he stood on duck-boards. A Royal Army Medical Corps corporal sat behind a trestle table.

'Who are you, then?' he asked him.

'Marine Doyle.'

'What d'you mean, *Marine?*'

'I mean Royal Marine Doyle, then.'

'Where were you?'

'Rangoon, Force Viper.'

'Never heard of it.'

'Well, you have now. I walked out. I've

238

been walking for weeks, months. I need treatment, I've got malaria.'

'Sick parade's over.'

'There must be someone who can help me; Doyle persisted. 'I mean, you're a medical orderly. You can see I'm ill.'

'I see someone wearing odd clothes, no uniform, no boots, no cap. How do I know who you are. Got your paybook?'

'No.'

'Identity discs?'

'Lost those long ago.'

'You could be anyone.'

'But I'm not anyone.'

And then the frustration, the whole reaction of Doyle's trek north suddenly overcame him. He collapsed. When he came round he was wearing a pair of cotton pyjamas and lying on a strip of matting on duckboards in another tent. He had a grey army blanket to cover him and he was shivering. He did not know how long he had been there and he did not care. The whole tent was filled with soldiers, wounded or suffering from fevers or dysentery.

'You've got a dose, a bad dose,' an orderly explained. 'Malaria. We can't do much for you here. But we'll move you out.'

'Where to?'

'Margherita.'

'How do I get there? Not walk, for goodness' sake. Not walk.'

'No. There's a tea plantation near here. They've got their own railway. We'll get you out on that. There are several others going with you.'

'When?'

'Soon as we can. Probably first light tomorrow.'

Doyle was issued with an army shirt and a new pair of shorts. The shirt had belonged to a sergeant, and his badge of rank, three chevrons in white tape, were still sewn on the sleeves. No one suggested removing them and Doyle did not bring up the matter. He had been a marine for a long time; now he would try his chances as a sergeant.

The plantation railway was narrow gauge, not unlike the miniature railways for children to ride on Doyle had seen at the seaside when he was a boy. Usually the trucks carried tea. Now they carried patients. Some, with head wounds and bandages around their eyes, had to be led to them. Others were carried or helped. Doyle walked. They sat or lay in silence: there seemed no point in exchanging names. They would split up again as soon as they reached Margherita. Here there was another tented hospital, but with more doctors and some nurses. Every tent was filled, with civilian refugees as well as servicemen.

After a few days here Doyle was again

moved, this time aboard a riverboat to a third tented camp. He still felt desperately ill. Sometimes he was not completely certain whether he was conscious or unconscious. Voices rose and receded. He found himself answering questions as though by rote, but it seemed that his voice belonged to another man; he felt somehow outside himself, simply watching all this, an observer, personally uninvolved.

In this camp he again lay on duckboards, and he knew his condition was worsening. The pain from his ankles became excruciating; his head ached and a hammer seemed to be pounding at the base of his skull. He endured this for as long as he could, and then, desperate for a remedy, he crawled out of his tent. Stumbling blindly along in the rain, he found a tent with a stake driven into the ground by the entrance door bearing two initials, MO. Doyle put his head through the opening. The medical officer inside looked at him in amazement. Doyle saw the doctor's lips move to form a question, but he did not hear the question, nor did he answer it, because he fell to the ground unconscious.

When he came round, he was in bed beneath a mosquito net. A nurse – who he was delighted to learn came from Darlington – was taking his temperature.

'Spinal malaria,' she said. 'Nasty, but

we've caught it in time.'

'How long will I be here?' Doyle asked her weakly. 'I must get back to headquarters.'

He could not bear any more delays: he had been months on the march.

'Of course, of course,' the nurse replied soothingly. 'You won't be here very long actually. We can only patch up people here. Then they move on.'

'Where to?'

'To a hospital nearer Calcutta, run by an American mission. You'll have Chinese nurses there.'

'I'd rather have you.'

'Flattery gets you everywhere,' retorted the nurse. 'Except here. Now, open your mouth and let's see what that temperature is doing.'

Whatever it was doing, it was not doing much for Doyle.

Days later he was again in a railway truck with other sick and wounded passengers. This time the train pulled into a station where army vehicles were waiting to take them to the American mission hospital. The nurses were Chinese nuns. While Doyle's injuries were being dressed, he could hear off-duty nurses singing hymns in the chapel next to his ward. He found something intensely soothing in hearing the familiar hymns Rock of Ages and Abide with Me. Truly, he believed, God had been with him on his long march.

After a week he was told he was fit enough to move. The shirt with the sergeant's stripes had been removed. So had his revolver; no arms were allowed in any military hospital. An American surgeon heard that he had no kit whatsoever and found him a pair of blue rubber polo boots, two sizes too large for Doyle usually, but ideal now to fit over his bandages. The surgeon also found him an American army shirt and a pair of shorts.

'Where are you heading for?' the orderly in charge of arrivals and departures asked him. 'What's your unit?'

'I'm not sure. I'm a marine, seemingly the only one in this area.'

'All Army guys are going up to Calcutta, to a transit camp, if that's any use to you. They get sorted out there.'

'I'll take that too,' said Doyle.

'Right. A truck is leaving in an hour. Nice to know you. Have a nice day.'

'And you,' said Doyle, impressed by his reception and his treatment. Now to headquarters, wherever that might be...

In due time the truck deposited him, with thirty others, at the army transit camp in Calcutta. It was dark when he arrived. The others on the draft had kitbags or packs; all possessed the basic necessities of service life: an AB64, the army book issued to every

243

soldier; a razor, comb, and lather-brush; a mess tin, with a knife, fork and spoon. Doyle had none of these items, not even a hat.

The new arrivals were documented by the light of a hurricane lamp in a tent. Rain cascaded down. The tent roof sagged. Where a lake of water had collected above the saturated canvas, this dripped through continually into buckets placed strategically on the floor.

'Who are you?' the army corporal asked Doyle.

'Doyle, Royal Marines.'

He wondered how many more times he would have to explain.

'Where's your gear then?'

'I haven't got any.'

'No bloody kit? Paybook?'

'I haven't got it.'

'Who the hell are you then?'

'I've told you.'

At that moment a sergeant came in out of the rain to see what the discussion was about. Doyle explained.

'We'll sort you out in the morning,' the sergeant promised him. Then, to the corporal: 'Give him two blankets and get him out of here. We haven't got all night.'

'Where am I going?' asked Doyle.

'With the rest.'

'What is this place? Where are they going?'

'It's not the bloody Ritz here, mate,' said the corporal belligerently. 'It's Calcutta racecourse. We've taken over the grandstand. You'll have to lie down on a bench there until we get you sorted out. You'll have a strip of mosquito net. Wrap it about your head to stop the mossies biting you.'

'A bit late for that. I've just had spinal malaria.'

'This will stop you getting it again. You can catch it half a dozen times. I've had malaria twice,' retorted the corporal.

Doyle went out into the wet darkness to find a spare space on a bench. Like a dosser, he thought. Still, he was nearer headquarters than he had been last night, but still not close enough, and still not quickly enough.

Next morning he borrowed a razor, a bar of soap and a lather-brush from someone and shaved and washed. He did not possess a towel, so he dried his face on his shirt. At breakfast he joined a queue at the end of a table under a canvas roof. The table was piled with plates and knives and forks. A cook standing behind the table slapped some scrambled egg and toast on his plate, and he collected an enamel mug of tea. He was cheered by the food, and also by the sight of friends: Wilf Mannion, a pre-war professional footballer who had played for Middlesbrough and also for England, and another man who had been in the same class at St Patrick's, Teddy Russell. They were both on their way into Burma.

Doyle reported to the Company Office and asked if he could have an advance of pay and some proper kit. The familiar questions and answers were repeated, like a catechism.

'Where's your paybook?' the clerk asked him, looking up from his old upright Oliver typewriter.

'I haven't got one.'

'Then how do we know you're not in debt?'

'I've been in Burma for months, with no chance of spending anything. And before that I was in the Maldives, which are hardly the Golden Mile. Surely I can have *some* money, ten rupees even. I mean, that's only about twelve shillings. I need to buy some toothpaste, a bar of soap, and I want some kit, a towel, pants, socks. I'm wearing stuff I got given at a mission hospital. Cast-offs.'

'Sorry. Can't help you, mate. Not without a paybook.'

'Well, how can I get a paybook?'

'Your regimental office.'

'But I don't know where my regimental office is. I'm in the Marines.'

'Well, your nearest unit, then.'

'But where is my nearest bloody unit?'

'No need to swear at me, mate. I'm only

trying to help.'

'I'm not swearing at anyone, just at the system. According to you people here, I don't exist. I could stay here for ever.'

'You might be in a worse place than this, at that. Perhaps back in Burma, eh? Look, I can't waste all day, I've got work to do.'

He went back to his typing.

Doyle returned angrily to his space on the grandstand bench. Next day he borrowed another razor to shave and a towel from someone else. Then he saw the Sergeant who had come into the tent on the night of his arrival.

'Here, you!' said the Sergeant. 'What's-your-name?'

'Doyle, sarge.'

'I been looking for you.'

'You must be the only person here who's doing that.'

'No, I'm not. The Captain wants to see you.'

'And where is he?'

'I'll take you to him now. Been searching for you all morning, I have.'

The Captain sat in an office with a company clerk. He was probably in his thirties; plump, with a sallow face, not a man to whom Doyle felt immediately drawn.

'Now, where are you from?' asked the Captain. 'I heard you were a marine or something.'

'I am. I'm a Royal Marine, sir. With Force Viper in Burma.'

'Force Viper? Never heard of it.'

Doyle began to relate the story of HMS *Enterprise*, blowing up the oil refineries, the running battles in the Irrawaddy.

'I see,' said the Captain. 'Well, how did you get out?'

'I walked, sir.'

'You *what?*'

'Walked, sir.'

'Where's your kit?'

'It's lost, with my paybook.'

'Hmm, this is very awkward.'

'I know, sir. Especially for me.'

'Now don't take that tack. We're doing our best here. In any case, marines are the Navy's responsibility, and this is an Army camp.'

'But, sir, it's all part of the same thing, isn't it?'

'In the broadest sense, yes. But it's also a matter of administration. We cannot issue kit to someone not in the Army. You must see that?'

'But in that case, I could be going about naked, sir.'

'That's absurd. You're not naked. You'll have to get any new kit you need from the Navy. I don't know of any marines in Calcutta.'

'Where's the nearest naval headquarters, sir?'

'Well, there is a navy contingent here, but nothing to do with the Marines. I'd say your best bet is Bombay, or even Colombo. That's my guess.'

'But how do I get there, sir?'

'We'll send a signal first. See if they know anything about you.'

So Doyle went back to the grandstand. To find headquarters, and return to fight again, seemed further away than ever.

For the next few days acquaintances in the camp would take him into Calcutta and treat him to a beer, or eggs and chips. But they soon found themselves unable, or unwilling, to continue to subsidise his refreshments or entertainment.

Every morning and afternoon he asked at Company Office whether they had received a reply from naval headquarters in reply to the signal they had sent. Always the answer was a shake of the head. Doyle began to doubt whether any signal had ever been sent, but this was not the place or time to voice such thoughts.

Someone told him that there might be some marines in Fort William, near Calcutta, and Doyle scrounged a lift in a truck going into town. He went to Fort William, but no one there knew of any Royal Marines. Two Military Police corporals saw him and approached him.

'Who are you with?' they asked him.

'Royal Marines.'

'Where's your cap, then?'

'I have no cap.'

'Hullo, hullo. You look like a deserter to me, mate.'

'I look like who I am,' Doyle retorted.

He explained who he was, why he was there, and where he had been. The Military Policemen looked at each other and then shrugged their shoulders.

Calcutta was full of refugees and had its full quota of deserters busily integrating themselves into the complex underworld of the city. With thousands of refugees, plus American, British, Indian, West African, New Zealand, Australian, Canadian and Dutch troops, it was very easy for soldiers to slip away and start up in business in the black market. But, on reflection, Doyle looked too ill and too thin to be a black marketeer. There was also something about the hardness in his eye that made the policemen reluctant to press matters too far. They nodded him on his way.

Back to the camp he went, to make a formal request to see the Major in charge of postings. He wore a starched khaki drill uniform with brightly polished crowns of his rank on his epaulettes and sambur-skin shoes. He had a gold ring on the little finger of his left hand. Doyle explained who he was, where he wanted to go.

'I want to fight, sir. I want a posting back to headquarters, and then to get back into action. I don't like hanging about, doing nothing.'

'My dear fellow,' said the Major smoothly, 'I sympathize with you entirely, but there is nothing I can do. We're all in difficult positions here. I mean, there's nothing I'd like more than to have a crack at the Jap, but there it is. I have to accept my posting. I mean, I was in Burma before the war, you know. Flew my wife and children out when all this unpleasantness started. But I haven't heard from them since.'

'I'm sorry to hear that, sir,' said Doyle. 'But it doesn't help me to get back to the war.'

'No need to be truculent. That sort of behaviour I will not tolerate. I hear you've been making a bit of a nuisance of yourself, in any case. You've no paybook, and no kit. You'll just have to wait your turn. You'll get posted in due course.'

More days passed; more inertia; more time lost. Doyle put in a request to see the Camp Commandant. He explained the situation to him.

'Right,' said the Colonel. 'I'll get you out of here as soon as I can. We're fed up with you here, anyhow. Nothing but complaining. Where would we get if everyone complained like you?'

'They're not in the same situation, sir. Where will I be posted to? Bombay?'

The Colonel grunted and nodded a dismissal.

Doyle believed that the Colonel's non-committal reply was tantamout to saying he was being posted to Bombay.

Next day he saw on the noticeboard outside company office a typed list of postings, to report to Sealdah Station, Calcutta. There was his name and number. He was delighted; at last he was on his way to Bombay, although he still possessed neither kit nor money. The draft of twelve men were given a sealed tin between them. This contained smaller tins of bully beef and butter, jam, sugar, and milk, with some dry biscuits. The routine was to empty out these ingredients on the train, and when the train stopped at a station or a signal, one of their number would jump down and run along the track with the empty tin. Locomotives in India each had a small tap at one side of the engine from which boiling water could be drawn. They would fill the tin from this and bring it back. Tea, condensed milk and sugar would be thrown into the boiling water to make tea.

The carriage was a third-class coach with wooden seats around its four sides, and slatted luggage racks above. There was not enough room for all to sleep or lie on the seats, so some climbed up onto the racks and lay there. At one end of the carriage was a bathroom with a basin and shower. An oval hole gaped in the floor, with two raised pieces of metal on either side, the size and shape of a human footprint, for the basic needs of nature. The windows of the compartment were empty of glass. Children would run barefooted along the rails when the train slowed for a station, holding out begging bowls and crying: 'No poppa, no momma, backsheesh, sahib.'

The sun beat like a drum on the iron roofs of the coaches. Doors were pegged open and hot gritty dust blew in. Some men sat in the doorway, watching the landscape of paddy fields and villages unfold.

The Sergeant in charge of the draft offered Doyle a cigarette.

'What are you going to do in Gaya?' he asked him.

'Nothing,' Doyle replied. 'I'm going to Bombay.'

'Not on this train, you aren't. It's going to Gaya.'

'Where the hell's that?'

'Hundreds of miles away in North India. A staging post. We must be the only people going to it from this direction. Most come to it from Bombay, on their way to Calcutta and then Burma. We're going to join the permanent staff and look after the place.'

'You speak for yourself, Sarge. I'm not having any of that. I'm going to Bombay, find naval headquarters and then get myself back into the war. That's what we're here for, isn't it?'

'Listen, lad,' said the Sergeant, leaning towards Doyle in a conspiratorial way. Why don't you wake up – and grow up?'

'What do you mean?'

'Why don't you go on the run?'

'On the run? But I've been on the run for months.'

'I don't mean trekking through Burma to join up and go back again. That's madness. I mean properly on the run. Nobody knows who you are or what you are. You've proved that already. If I were in your shoes, I wouldn't be going to Gaya. I'd have got the hell out and gone into the black market. I know a friend in the Engineers who did that. He'll have made enough to retire on by the end of the war.'

'If the Japs invade India, he'll have nothing, never mind retiring,' retorted Doyle.

'They'll not get to Calcutta,' said the Sergeant.

'They will if too many take your advice. Anyhow, what could I do on the run in Calcutta?'

'I can put you on to people. We might even go together.'

'I think not,' said Doyle.

'You don't know what you're talking about, Doyle. Let me tell you something. I was walking down Chowringhee the other day and saw a bloody great American car coming towards me, a major driving. I looked at this and, blow me, the major was one of my old muckers. We'd been privates together at the depot in Canterbury. So I stepped out in the road, held out my hand, and he stopped.

'"What's the trouble, sergeant?" he asked, officer's tone of voice.

'I said, "Don't give me that, mate."

'"Shit!" he said, recognizing me. "Get inside."

'So I get in alongside him. We drive right down to the smart end of town, off Park Street, and stop by the side of a block of flats.

'I say, "Where are we going?" He says, "Home. To have a drink with me."

'I say, "Are you on the staff or something?"

'"Something," he says, and smiles.

'So we go upstairs. He's got a fine flat, air-conditioning, fridge full of booze, and an Indian servant, white mess jacket, pouring out drinks.

'I said, "How did you get all this? How are you a major and I am still only a sergeant?"

'"I'm not a bloody major," he says. "I'm not even a sergeant. I'm a private. I deserted.

I'm in with the Yanks here. The black market."

"'How haven't you been picked up?" I asked him.

"'Who's going to pick me up?" he asks me. "A couple of corporal redcaps? Rubbish!"

"'How d'you make the money, then?"

"'Easy,' he says. "There's been a great famine in Calcutta, now Burma's gone. Used to buy a lot of rice from Burma. Now there's nothing, people starving everywhere, dying in the streets, and the price of rice pegged to what the bearers and the coolies and the sweepers earn a month. That's about thirty rupees, plus a shack to live in.

"'Right. The whole economy in Bengal is geared to that level, all the prices. Everything. Then the Yanks come in. They say it's scandalous only paying these poor sods thirty chips a month. We'll pay 'em three hundred.

"'So they pay their bearers ten times what they were getting before. Great for them. But thousands of other poor devils are still only getting the thirty chips they've always had, and they can't cope, because the merchants who own the rice bump up the prices. That's why there are so many hundreds of thousands starving here. Instead of helping the Indians, the Yanks have helped half Bengal to starve. The road to hell is paved with good intentions. That's what they taught me in Sunday School when I was a kid.'"

'How did your friend come in?' Doyle asked him.

They provide transport to carry the rice from the godowns to the warehouses.'

'But where do they get the transport from?'

'The Army, of course. Say you have a colonel, a major and a couple of captains, all in crisp khaki drill, arriving in a jeep at some army dump full of 3-hundredweight trucks run by a second lieutenant. He's not going to query who they are, is he? He doesn't twig they're all deserters. Then they take their cut from the merchant. Sometimes they actually steal the stuff themselves.'

'Did you turn the man in?' Doyle asked.

'Of course not. Who'd believe me? But it made me think. We could go on the run together. You're a big bloke. If you have walked out of Burma, as you say, you must have some loaf. After all, you kept alive. Others didn't.'

'That's not for me,' replied Doyle. 'I just want to get to the nearest Marines head-quarters, be kitted out and take whatever active posting comes up.'

'You must be mad,' said the Sergeant despairingly, and turned away from him in disgust.

At Gaya a truck took the men to the camp.

The monsoon had restarted after a brief lull, and the camp was waterlogged. Their beds were charpoys, wooden frames with rope mattresses, and everything inside and outside the tents seemed to be under several inches of water.

Some earlier arrivals had found stones and brought them in and put them by the side of their beds, so that when they stood barefoot to dress, they could at least stand on the stones and not in water. An air of depression and sullen, bored misery hung over the whole camp.

Doyle sat on the edge of his bed, mosquitoes humming around his head, a hurricane lamp hanging from the centrefold of the tent, his feet in an empty ration tin to keep them dry; he feared that if they were soaked again, his wounds would reopen.

This was no place to stay. Doyle knew that if he joined the permanent staff at the camp, he would be kept there indefinitely. In fact, he would probably never be released for active service. He had met soldiers who had served for years in depots and transit camps, relieved that they faced almost no risk of action. He was not of that persuasion.

If he stayed, he would be interviewed and his name added to a nominal roll. He would be given a bed space, kit, and duties to perform, and from then on the future would stretch to an infinity of drudgery. He was a fighting man, a Royal Marine. This prospect had no attractions for him. The only thing to do was to leave now. Tomorrow could well be too late.

He made his decision and went out of the tent, nearly tripping over the guy ropes in the darkness. Rain was still pouring down. Under a few lamps placed high up on poles around the perimeter, the camp looked like a lake, with each tent a small canvas island. He approached the entrance. A sentry wore a shiny anti-gas cape around his shoulders against the downpour. A truck arrived with some stores, and another truck was waiting to go out. Doyle ran alongside the driver.

'Give us a lift, mate,' he said.

'Get in,' the driver replied, barely looking at him.

They drove in silence to the station. Here the driver backed into a siding. Doyle jumped down.

'Thanks, mate,' he said.

He needed to avoid the Military Transport Officer who shared a small office in the station with a sergeant to check troops arriving and departing. This was quite easy to do. Both men were in their office, sheltering from the rain. Doyle also kept away from the first-class waiting room, and the second-class waiting room; the fewer people who saw him the better. A handful of Indians, with piles of suitcases and cardboard boxes, stood on the platform, waiting for the train.

As soon as this was sighted, Doyle knew that hundreds more passengers, who were not even visible at that moment, would suddenly materialize from wherever they had been hiding against the rain and leap into it. There would not be room for all of them, so late arrivals would hang on outside, on to the doors, and on running-boards. Others more agile would climb up on to the roof and lie there, oblivious of the fact that if the train went under a low bridge they could be swept to death. That was their problem; Doyle felt he had enough of his own.

He kept in the shadow of the station building, avoiding the searching beams of headlights on cars and trucks arriving. When the signal lights by the track changed from red to green, he walked out on to the line. In the distance he heard the faint shriek of a whistle, then the train's searchlight appeared in the distance round a bend, growing brighter and brighter as it approached on the line where he stood. Hastily, he jumped from one set of rails to another.

The train came in, a huge engine with its cowcatcher. An angry red glow from the furnace lit up the cab with the glare of an inferno. It reminded him of the little engine he had helped to stoke on its way through North Burma, and he wondered where that was now, what had happened to those who had travelled on it with him, and the others who had followed the padre.

The train stopped with a shriek of brakes and a roar of escaping steam, as he had intended, between him and the platform. He climbed up on to the running-board, let himself into a compartment and sat down. It was a dimly lit second-class compartment and seemed full of troops. The air was thick with cigarette smoke.

No one else entered or left. Those already there had been sleeping, and some, awake, looked at him without interest or surprise. It was nothing unusual for someone to board a train from the unexpected side.

Doyle sat quietly, not speaking. The train started, and the man next to him offered him a cigarette.

'Where are you from, then? What's your mob?' he enquired.

'Royal Marines,' said Doyle.

'Didn't know we'd got any out here, so far from the sea.'

'That's why I'm glad to be going back to the sea,' said Doyle. 'Bombay.'

'Bombay?' shouted someone else. 'You must be bloody mad.'

'Why? Should be there tomorrow.'

'Not on this train you won't. It's going to Calcutta.'

'You're joking.'

'About Calcutta? I should be so lucky. We've just *come* from Bombay. The train only stopped here to pick up mail apparently. The Bombay mail train is due any minute.'

'We're going to Calcutta?' repeated Doyle, bemused.

'That's right.'

There was the sudden roaring shriek of another whistle, and an express thundered past, feet away from the window, on the other track.

'That's the Bombay train. You got on the wrong one.'

Doyle said nothing; he felt beyond speech. He must have become disorientated when the driver reversed his truck, and had assumed the next train must be for Bombay. The assumption had been wrong. He lit the cigarette the man had given him, and in the crowded compartment remained alone with his thoughts. When the train pulled into Calcutta, the soldiers in the compartment now looked at Doyle quizzically.

'You got no kit, then?' one asked him.

'Nothing.'

'On the run, are you?'

'Exactly what I'm not.' retorted Doyle. 'But, because I'm a marine, the Army won't deal with me. When I reach Bombay, the Navy will take care of everything.'

'You'll have to get past the redcaps in Calcutta first.'

'Not necessarily,' said someone else. There's a Salvation Army canteen in the station. Go in there and find out when the Bombay train leaves. You can probably bluff your way past the barrier without ever leaving the station, never see a bloody redcap.'

This is what Doyle did. He fell in with the others, humping their kitbags along the platform, to the canteen. He had no money to buy a cup of tea or a bun, but sitting at one of the round tables were half-a-dozen men he had seen in the racecourse camp in Calcutta. They greeted him with ironic cheers.

'You should be in Bombay,' they said.

'I should be,' he agreed, 'but I got on the wrong train. Any idea what platform the Bombay train is?'

'We should have. We're catching it. But not all the way to Bombay. We get off about fifty miles this side.'

'Have you got warrants?' Doyle asked.

'Sure,' said a Corporal. 'You fall in behind us. We'll give you a bit of kit to carry. No one will check you. Meantime, I suppose you've no money?'

'Dead right. None.'

So they bought him tea and a poached egg on toast. He drank and ate thankfully, had a wash, combed his hair, and when they were ready, went out with them to the main part of the station. They walked as a group. One lent him a bush hat; another, a pack; and they all went through the barrier without anyone checking them.

'The only snag you'll meet on the journey is when the ticket wallah comes round,' the Corporal explained, as they climbed into the compartment. 'You leave him to me.'

'Glad to,' Doyle replied thankfully.

It was a long journey; troop trains took several days to cross India. For much of the way, Doyle sat on the floor in the doorway, with his feet out on the running-board, watching the drab, vast countryside, soaked with rain, slide past, as it had done on the way to Gaya.

When the train stopped at stations, the sellers of Indian sweetmeats, balancing on their heads baskets of sticky sweets on leaves, and the charwallahs offering metal beakers of tea, paraded up and down the platform crying their wares. Doyle and others on the train, civilians and troops alike, also stepped down onto the platform, to walk a few yards to stretch their legs.

Doyle felt he could not scrounge on the generosity and good will of these men, so he became adept at being last back on the train. As it started to move, he would seize a cake or a chapatti from one of the vendors, and then jump back on to the train with it. The man would run after him, crying for his money, shouting abuse, until the train gathered speed. Doyle did not like taking food from these people, but in the circumstances he felt he had no option: his need seemed at least as great as theirs.

When the ticket collector came along the train from carriage to carriage, he examined the rail warrant and counted the men against the number of the warrant.

'One extra,' he declared, and pointed to Doyle trying to keep out of sight on the top bunk.

'That's a mate of ours,' said the Corporal.

'I am knowing that. But where is the warrant of this mate? That is what I am asking you.'

The Corporal shook his head gravely.

'Don't ask him. He's suffering from a terrible disease. No cure.

'What is it you mean? The pox?'

'Worse,' said the Corporal gloomily. 'Go too near him and you'll catch it. Die within weeks.'

'So why, I am asking, why haven't you caught it?'

'We've been inoculated against it, that's why. Army doctors. Civvy doctors just can't get hold of the special drugs.'

The ticket collector took another look at Doyle, who groaned realistically. The man moved away smartly and did not return. The draft reached their destination, and climbed out on to the platform with their kit. Doyle was left alone in the compartment until it trundled into Victoria Station, Bombay. Before it did so, he went into the little lavatory compartment, washed his face in the metal basin, and examined his reflection critically in the mirror.

He hardly recognized himself. He had momentarily forgotten that he had a beard and was hollow-eyed. His face had been burned almost black with the sun. He still wore the shirt, shorts, and polo boots that the American surgeon had provided, and he still possessed nothing to prove who he really was: no paybook; his name was not on any nominal roll. Nothing. He put his face in the cold water for a moment, trying to cool himself and compose his thoughts.

As soon as the train stopped, he jumped down on to the platform. This was packed with people; luggage was being unloaded in great quantities. He had never seen so many people in such a confined space before; refugees from Burma; civilian families travelling; troops. He threaded his way through the crowds, out to the main part of the station. Here he could see military policemen walking in pairs, watching for deserters or service men or women who they considered were improperly dressed.

They would almost certainly pick on him, because he did not look like a civilian nor yet a soldier. His appearance marked him as someone they would wish to question. He determined to avoid this risk and moved away from the main gates. He saw some advertisement hoardings on one side, glanced over his shoulder to make sure the policemen were not coming in his direction, and then, as quickly as he could, he shinned up a hoarding and dropped down on the other side.

He was out on a street with buses and cars trundling past and horse-drawn gharries with lacquered black hoods up against the sun. Rickshaw wallahs padded up and down and looked at him hopefully.

Doyle walked along the pavement, not knowing where to go or even where exactly he was. At a crossroads he saw a naval petty officer standing by a corner booth that displayed a selection of garish Indian vernacular magazines. He approached him. The petty officer looked at him enquiringly, wondering who this apparition was and what business he sought with him.

'I'm Marine Doyle,' Doyle explained. 'I want you to take me to the Navy office.'

'You are *who?*' the petty officer asked him. 'Are you an Indian?'

'No, British. A Plymouth marine.'

'Why are you dressed like this, then?'

'It's a long story,' said Doyle. 'I've come out of Burma. I was in a landing party off *Enterprise.*'

'*Enterprise?*' repeated the petty officer.

267

'She's lying in the bay now.

'That's lucky for me,' replied Doyle. 'Someone aboard will be able to remember the landing party in Rangoon.'

'You a marine – dressed like that?'

'Yes.'

'What's the motto of the Royal Marines?'

'Per mare, per terram. By land, by sea,' replied Doyle. 'I reckon I've lived it.'

'Well, maybe you're right. You'd better come with me.'

He marched Doyle through the streets to the Navy office overlooking the harbour. A Master-at-Arms was sitting behind a counter with a mug of tea. The petty officer whispered to him.

'This bloke here says he's a marine.'

The Master-at-Arms nodded slowly. He had heard many strange stories in his time. Was this another?

He turned to Doyle.

'Now, son, what's going on? Who are you, exactly?' he asked, not unkindly.

Doyle thought: 'Here we go again.'

He took a deep breath.

'I walked out of Burma.'

'You what?'

'I walked out of Burma. I've no money, no papers. Nothing but what I'm wearing.'

The petty officer interrupted.

'He says he came off *Enterprise* in Rangoon.'

'She's in the bay now,' said the Master-at-Arms.

'I've told him.'

'They'll vouch for me there,' said Doyle. We all got cut up and left.'

'Why did *Enterprise* leave you?'

'I don't know, but she did. I've walked about 500 miles, and I want to get back into action, and no one will listen to me. And another thing, I'm bloody hungry.'

'Well,' said the Master-at-Arms, 'You'll have to see the officer. He'll be here around ten o'clock. You can tell your story to him. It's a damned odd story, though, isn't it?'

'Agreed,' said Doyle. 'But it's true.'

They put him in a room with two sailors, and he sensed he was in some kind of open arrest: he might run amok or steal something. They also gave him a cup of tea and a slice of bread with butter and jam.

At ten o'clock he was marched out in front of the officer. Again the questioning began. Why had he no cap? Why was he unshaven and improperly dressed? Where was his paybook?

'Do you mean to say you actually left the fighting in Burma?'

'That's right, sir. If I hadn't, I wouldn't have got here, would I?'

'You're a deserter, then?'

'No, sir. There was nothing else to do. My orders were to make for headquarters, get kitted out, and fight again. I couldn't do that if I was a prisoner, or if I was dead.'

'Damned odd story,' said the officer.

At that moment there was a discreet knock on the door. A marine entered the room. Doyle looked at him in amazement, a surprise that was shared by the marine, for he was Jacky Simm, who came from Newcastle-upon-Tyne and who had been in Force Viper with him. Simm had been flown out from Myitkyina. Recognition was immediate, and with it the atmosphere changed.

'We'll get you sorted out,' the officer assured Doyle.

Within hours they had. A signal was sent to Ceylon, which was the last naval base to which he had been attached, and records there identified his name and number. They thought he was dead; he was actually listed as 'Reported Missing, Believed Killed.'

The Master-at-Arms gave him a hat, boots, shorts and shaving kit.

'I'd like some money, too,' said Doyle.

'We've no record of how much you're owed,' said the Master-at-Arms cautiously.

'So how much can I have? I must be owed quite a bit.'

'We can let you have ten rupees.'

This was the equivalent of about 12 shillings, sixty pence in today's currency.

He was billeted in the Apollo Hotel, which

had been taken over by the Navy while they decided what to do with him. He received medical treatment for his legs, and at last, months after the wounds had been inflicted, they began to heal. For a job only until he was fit, they assured him – he helped sort mail in the naval office into pigeon holes, to be taken out to different ships in the bay. Sometimes he took it out himself.

Weeks passed without any word of a posting back to Burma. The thought occurred to him that, instead of waiting for an answer to his repeated requests to be kitted out and sent back to Burma in a fighting unit, it might be more productive of results to stow away on a British-bound troopship and seek an active service posting from the Royal Marines barracks in Plymouth. Perhaps there they would listen to his request more sympathetically – and act on it?

Although he toyed with this idea, because it held certain undeniable attractions, he felt that this could also be misconstrued as running away, and he had not marched so far or endured so much to run away now. As Major Johnston had stressed: 'You never win by retreating.'

So he stayed where he was, until one day he collapsed with a relapse of malaria. He was sent to St George's Hospital, and here a visitor, Mrs Seddon, the wife of an oil company director, who had organized a convalescent home for sailors outside Bombay, took him into her care. She ran a former convent, apparently at her own expense, helping sailors and marines recovering from wounds or illnesses. She also arranged for Doyle to send a telegram to his parents: *Safe and well. Don't worry. Doyle.*

Doctors visited recuperating patients twice a week, and they were immediately concerned about the condition of Doyle's ankles and feet. Although the edges of the wounds had joined, the scars were large, and the legs were still badly swollen. The skin had changed colour and was now florid, and in places purple. He was sent before a medical board. They reached their verdict very quickly.

'You'll never march far with those legs, Doyle.'

'They'll get better, sir,' Doyle assured them.

'Eventually. But it's amazing you haven't lost your legs altogether. It's only your strong constitution that has saved them – and you.'

'They carried me a long way, sir.'

'And now they'll carry you a longer way still,' replied the senior examining surgeon. 'All the way back to the UK for treatment.'

When he heard this news, Doyle tried to obtain a Royal Marine's uniform suitable for winter wear in Britain, but no one could help him. At last he went to the Indian Naval Dockyard, where an Indian tailor made him a marine's suit in blue. The cloth was rather finer than the general issue, and the trousers did not have the red piping of a Royal Marine. However, the tailor had a number of Royal Marine brass buttons, and sewed these on.

Feeling rather like an actor playing the part of a Royal Marine in a stage uniform, Doyle, and others ill and wounded and declared beyond any medical or surgical treatment that India could offer, were mustered aboard a merchant ship. The ship was due to reach Liverpool in November and Doyle lacked a greatcoat. A Bombay newspaper, however, was promoting a scheme to give away sheepskin jackets to people who might not possess warm clothes and were being repatriated to Britain. Doyle presented himself to the newspaper office and was given one, plus a balaclava woollen helmet and a pair of leather gauntlets. Aboard the ship, Doyle realized that this hardly constituted the accepted uniform for a Royal Marine, so he exchanged these items for a dark blue waterproof raincoat owned by a sailor.

The ship sailed under escort to Cape Town, and then on her own to Freetown. Several of the crew deserted at Cape Town rather than face the journey north without an escort or in the relative safety of a convoy.

At the last moment, as the ship was ready to sail, and mooring ropes had been cast off, several of these men followed it in a small boat, hoping to be re-engaged, but the Captain refused to take them aboard. This meant he was short of crew to work the ship, so all troops who were fit enough were asked to help out on watches and with other tasks.

On the trip, Doyle played bingo with some success, and this meant he landed at Liverpool with several pounds in his pocket.

At Lime Street station they were fallen into ranks, according to their destinations. The train for Plymouth was not due to leave until midnight – a wait of more than eight hours – and until it left, all troops were forbidden to leave the station.

The sailor whose raincoat Doyle had exchanged for his sheepskin jacket now approached him.

'My home is in Bootle, not very far from here,' he explained. 'What do you say to coming back home with me? We can easily be back here by midnight before the train goes.'

'I'm game,' said Doyle. 'But how can we get out?'

'Leave that to me.'

A truck that had delivered newspapers at the station was reversing in the yard. The sailor approached the driver.

'Can you give us a lift out Bootle way?' he asked him.

'I'm going near there,' the driver replied. 'Hop in the back.'

The driver dropped them in the main street and then went on. Doyle and the sailor were surprised to see huge crowds of people were lining both sides of the road. Most of them were women.

'What's happening here?' Doyle asked a policeman.

'The King and Queen. They're visiting the Town Hall, just up the road. All these women are war workers given time off to see them.'

Doyle and the sailor joined the crowd. Suddenly, as the King and Queen walked down the Town Hall steps, the sailor saw his mother across the road, and shouted: *'Mum!'*

She looked at him in amazement. She had not expected him to come home, and they embraced ecstatically, with the King and Queen behind them, and everyone cheering. Doyle sprang to attention and saluted as the King passed within a few feet.

Later, Doyle, the sailor, his mother, father, sisters, brothers, and neighbours, went to the nearest pub to celebrate the homecoming.

Somehow, without remembering exactly how, he returned to Lime Street station and was put on the train.

On the journey south, two other marines joined the train, which reached Plymouth late on Sunday morning. A Royal Marines truck was waiting in the forecourt to collect stores, and the driver gave the three of them a lift as far as one end of Stonehouse Street, near the barracks. They set off to walk the remaining distance, and as they walked, they heard the sounds of martial music behind them, growing steadily louder.

They looked at each other in surprise, and then Doyle remembered: it was Sunday morning, and this would be church parade marching back behind the band. The parade overtook them just outside the barracks. The other two marines went into the barracks just in front of them, but Doyle waited to watch the magnificent procession, as, in pipe-clayed helmets, and brass ablaze, the band led the detachment through the barrack gates.

Doyle had no kit to carry, and dressed in his blue raincoat, with his strange Indian cap and uniform, he fell in almost instinctively behind the rear marker. This was how his journey should end, he felt; marching triumphantly back into headquarters, *his* headquarters, Plymouth Royal Marines barracks.

But as he approached the gates, a Corporal of the guard halted him.

'Who are you, mate? Where d'you think you're going?'

'Marine Doyle,' he replied, 'reporting for duty.'

'But where are you from? Why are you dressed up in this gear? A civvy raincoat and that?'

'I'm from Force Viper, Corporal,' Doyle replied.

'Force Viper? Last I heard of them was in Burma, thousands of miles away.'

Other members of the guard had come out of the guardroom and stood staring at Doyle, suspecting a hoax, a joker, perhaps a lunatic escaped from an asylum.

'That's right, Corporal. I may be the only survivor – but I was told to make my own way back to headquarters, and here I am.'

The Corporal turned to the others. They shrugged. No one quite knew what to say. Doyle looked military enough in his bearing, but his uniform was distinctly unusual, and so was his raincoat.

'Into the guardroom, then,' the Corporal decided, 'till we sort this one out.'

The other two marines were already being interviewed by the sergeant. Both had come back on leave; there were no problems concerning them. Then came Doyle's turn. He gave his name and number.

'Where are you from?' asked the Sergeant.

'Burma, Sergeant.'

The Sergeant looked at him quizzically.

'What were you doing in Burma?'

Doyle looked at the Sergeant in amazement.

'I was fighting. What do you think I was doing?'

'Marines in Burma?' said the Sergeant. 'I don't know of any marines in Burma.'

'You wouldn't, would you, sitting there?'

'Wait a minute, son. *What* force did you say you were with?'

'Force Viper.'

'Never heard of it.'

'Well, the Corporal's heard of it.'

'That don't prove a thing. Where's your kit?'

'In Burma.'

'Where's your rifle?'

'In Burma.'

'How did you get here?'

'I walked to India, reached Bombay, and finally I've arrived here. I've been on the go for months, and I'm hungry and I'm tired and I want a wash.'

'Oh,' said the Sergeant. 'Well, we'll have to look into this. Which company were you in?'

'I joined up in R company,' said Doyle. 'Recruits company.'

'You joined up here, did you?'

'Yes.'

Where did you go from here, then?

'First of all, I went to Portsmouth, and then on a gunnery course. I went to Fort Cumberland.'

'I'll get you a cup of tea,' said the Sergeant. Then we'll go round the companies and see what's what.'

They visited R company first. No one knew anything about Marine Doyle there. All the recruits had long since gone to their units, and the permanent staff had changed. To them he was just another stranger.

They went on to A company, B company, C company. No one had heard of Doyle. The Sergeant was baffled. He arranged for Doyle to have a wash and a meal, and Doyle was sitting on a bed in a barrack room when the tannoy crackled: 'Marine Doyle to report at once to the main office.'

So he went to the main office, and to his surprise found it full of officers.

'Sit down,' said a Captain, as Doyle saluted.

'Now,' said the Captain, 'in your own time, tell us where you came from and all the rest of it.'

Doyle started to tell his story once more. Halfway through, an orderly came in with a sheaf of papers. The Captain glanced at them.

'We've found your papers. They are in a file, "Missing, Believed Killed." We thought you were dead. Now, we'll get you home as soon as possible. There's a train going from North Road Station at four o'clock. We'll give you a warrant.'

They also gave Doyle £40. He went back to the barrack room to sit on the bed until he left for the station. But there was a final delay. A medical orderly came in and told him he was to report to the Royal Naval Hospital at Plymouth.

'But there's nothing wrong with me,' Doyle protested.

'You're going to hospital, mate. That's all there is to it. Orders.'

So, very reluctantly, Doyle went into the hospital. He had to discard his uniform, because the custom then was to dress new patients in any uniform that might be available, but not their own. He was given the uniform of a petty officer without badges of rank. This had belonged to a man who was probably six inches shorter than Doyle, and it only fitted where it touched.

For several days he was kept in hospital. Every morning he had to stand by his bed when the medical officers and matron came round the ward. Finally, Doyle was told to report to the surgeon commander. If he declared him fit, he could then go home on leave.

'I can't report to him in this ridiculous rig,' Doyle protested.

'You'll have to, mate,' said the orderly.

'But I'm like a bloody scarecrow. I've got my own stuff, can't I put it on?'

'Against the rules.'

Doyle was marched out to see the surgeon commander, who looked at him in horror and annoyance.

'Don't you know you have to be properly dressed?' he asked Doyle. This is as much a parade as anything else.'

'I agree, sir. But this is all they'll let me wear.'

Doyle was immediately given back his uniform and a promise to catch the next train to Middlesbrough. When he arrived there at about eight o'clock on the following morning, he was astonished to see that the station had been bombed. The Leeds Hotel, which he remembered standing outside it, had been completely destroyed.

He walked up through the familiar streets to Mills Street. As he entered this road, he was horrified to see that one side of it had been totally flattened by bombs – and this was the side where he lived. From the end of the road, he could not see his house. His heart started to flutter in horror. Had he come back all this way to find no one in his family left alive?

But as he drew closer, he saw that the damage stopped two houses from his. He went up to the front door, and knocked on it. His mother opened the door. She was so astonished at seeing him that she did not even greet him, but rushed across the street to a friend's house shouting: 'He's home! He's home!'

She kept staring at him as though he were a ghost. His father was working on the six o'clock morning shift and was not due home until after two. At first, Doyle thought he would go down to the factory, Britannia Works, and meet him. Then he decided to wait at home until he returned.

His father came in at the front door, saw his son, and could not believe he was actually there. Both parents had good reason for their surprise. They had received his cable from Bombay, signed simply 'Doyle.' But they had been told months earlier by the Royal Marines office that he was missing, believed killed, and they thought that this cable must have been sent by his brother, who was serving in the Army.

After leave at home, Doyle returned to Plymouth barracks. His wounds had outwardly healed, but he was never passed fit for any further active service. He assisted in training marines for D-day, and he served for another four years in the Corps, always in Britain.

Sometimes, in the years between then and now, perhaps on an unusually hot day in summer, or in winter when rain on the roof wakes him up, William Doyle will remember his long solitary march north through Burma, and the people he met, and he will wonder who survived and who failed to make the border.

He also wonders what happened to other individuals he met on the way: the sergeant on the train to Gaya; the priest in Myitkyina; the padre who left the train; the boy he helped with bottles of aspirin; the woman and her party who he led over the rope bridge. Perhaps, too, they have also wondered what happened to the Marine from Mandalay who so briefly entered their lives and then went on his way alone.

One thing William Doyle has learned: all experience, however irrelevant it may seem at the time, can play an important, even vital, part in every life. Time spent in reconnaissance is never wasted.

If Doyle had not learned that moss grows on the north side of trees, he could have lost his way.

If he had not been willing to fall on his knees and pray, as he had learned as a child, he might never have found a path out of the jungle.

If he had not undergone a course in lifting gun barrels using pulleys and tripod, how many refugees of all ages and races might have died on the far side of an unknown river?

It is always easy to look back and think what one could have done, maybe should have done. As he says, 'Everyone has twenty-twenty hindsight. The most important thing is to do what you think is best at the time and stick by your decision, no matter what others may think or say.'

Through his training, his example, his courage, William Doyle saved the lives of unnumbered refugees with physical help and moral example.

In a war to destroy life, he saved it. And in attempting to find his headquarters, the Marine from Mandalay found something even more important. He found himself.

BIBLIOGRAPHY

SITTANG by Louis Allen (Arrow Books)
DISTINCTLY I REMEMBER: a personal story of Burma by Harold Braund MBE, MC. (Wren Publishing Pty)
FIGHTING MAD by Michael Calvert (Jarrolds)
PRISONERS OF HOPE by Michael Calvert (Jonathan Cape)
THE LONGEST RETREAT: The Burma Campaign 1942 by Tim Carew (Hamish Hamilton)
DESPERATE JOURNEY by Francis Clifford (Hodder and Stoughton)
RANGOON TO KOHIMA by Terence Dillon (Regimental Headquarters, The Gloucestershire Regiment)
BURMA by F S V Donnison (Ernest Benn)
THE STORY OF BURMA by F Tennyson Jesse (Macmillan)
LIFE IN THE BURMESE JUNGLE by A A Lawson (The Book Guild)
A HELL OF A LICKING: The Retreat from Burma 1941-42 by James Lunt (Collins)
THE RETREAT FROM BURMA: An Intelligence Officer's Personal Story by Lt Col Tony Mains, late 9th Gurkha Rifles (W

Foulsham & Co.)

TALES OF BURMA by Alister McCrae and friends (James Paton of Paisley)

ESCAPE FROM THE RISING SUN: The Incredible Voyage of the Sederhana Djohanis by Ian Skidmore (Leo Cooper)

THE WAR by Louis L Snyder (Bell Publishing Co.) New York

...AND SOME FELL BY THE WAYSIDE: An Account of the North Burma Evacuation by A R Tainsh (Orient Longmans)

FORGOTTEN FRONTIER by Geoffrey Tyson (W H Targett & Co.)

THE WAR AGAINST JAPAN, Vols. 2 and 3 (HM Stationery Office)

Archive material: Reference 7/19/2(5) from the Royal Marines Museum.